The anthropology of justice

Law has often been seen as a relatively autonomous domain, one in which a professional elite sharply controls the impact of broader social relations and cultural concepts. By contrast this study asserts that the analysis of legal systems, like the analysis of social systems generally, requires an understanding of the concepts and relationships encountered in everyday social life. Using as its substantive base the Islamic law courts of Morocco, the study explores the cultural basis of judicial discretion. From the proposition that in Arabic culture relationships are subject to considerable negotiation the idea is developed that the shaping of facts in a court of law, the use of local experts, and the organization of the judicial structure all contribute to the reliance on local concepts and personnel to inform the range of judicial discretion. By drawing comparisons with the exercise of judicial discretion in America the study demonstrates that cultural concepts deeply inform the evaluation of issues and the shape of a judge's decision.

The Anthropology of Justice is not only the first full-scale study of the actual operations of a modern Islamic law court anywhere in the Arab world but a demonstration of the theoretical basis on which a cultural analysis of the law may be founded.

THE LEWIS HENRY MORGAN LECTURES/1985

presented at
The University of Rochester
Rochester, New York

Lewis Henry Morgan Lecture Series

IX. 18—THE KADI, WITH MUFTI ATTENDING

Engraving of a qadi and attendant scholars, from an original design by William Harvey, in Edward Lane, *The Thousand and One Nights*, vol. II (London: Chatto and Windus, 1889), p. 568.

The anthropology of justice
Law as culture in Islamic society

LAWRENCE   ROSEN
Princeton University

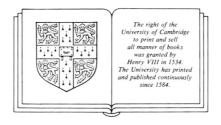

The right of the
University of Cambridge
to print and sell
all manner of books
was granted by
Henry VIII in 1534.
The University has printed
and published continuously
since 1584.

CAMBRIDGE UNIVERSITY PRESS

CAMBRIDGE
NEW YORK   NEW ROCHELLE
MELBOURNE   SYDNEY

Published by the Press Syndicate of the University of Cambridge
The Pitt Building, Trumpington Street, Cambridge CB2 1RP
32 East 57th Street, New York, NY 10022, USA
10 Stamford Road, Oakleigh, Melbourne 3166, Australia

© Cambridge University Press 1989

First published 1989

Printed in Great Britain at the University Press, Cambridge

British library cataloguing in publication data
Rosen, Lawrence, 1941–
The anthropology of justice: law as
culture in Islamic society.—(The Lewis
Henry Morgan lectures).
1. Anthropological perspectives
I. Title   II. Series
340′.115

Library of Congress cataloguing in publication data
Rosen, Lawrence, 1941–
The anthropology of justice: law as culture in Islamic society/
Lawrence Rosen.
p.   cm. – (The Lewis Henry Morgan lectures: 1985)
Bibliography.
Includes index.
ISBN 0 521 36513 9.   ISBN 0 521 36740 9 (pbk.)
1. Islamic law.   2. Law and anthropology.   I. Title.   II. Series.
LAW
340.5′9 – dc 19   88–21438   CIP

ISBN 0 521 36513 9   hard covers
ISBN 0 521 36740 9   paperback

For Mary Beth

Contents

Foreword

Lewis Henry Morgan, in whose honor this lecture series was established, never attempted to develop an approach to law commensurate with his contributions to the study of kinship. Yet his training as a lawyer clearly had consequences in various aspects of his work, and recent developments in the anthropology of law would surely have intrigued him.

Professor Rosen delivered the 1985 Lewis Henry Morgan Lectures on March 19, 21, 26, and 28, and the present volume is an expanded and revised version of his lectures. Since Professor Rosen is one of those working on the anthropology of law who has been trained in both disciplines, his work repays careful attention, for he has developed an approach that integrates the two specialities. Here, he demonstrates the value of such an integrative approach when it is used to examine Islamic law. By considering particular personal status cases brought before a qadi (judge) in a small Moroccan town, Professor Rosen is able to illuminate hitherto obscure points with regard to Islamic law and procedure. He is also able to show how closely related the law and the court are to many other aspects of Moroccan society and culture.

Professor Rosen's work cannot easily be categorized as belonging to one or another tradition in either anthropology or law. What he has to say frequently bears on issues of importance, both older and more recent, in these fields. These include such diverse concerns as Malinowski's (or Bourdieu's) emphasis on context, Mauss's and Fortes' discussion of the person and personhood, and Austin's performative utterances. These and other matters are, however, here subordinate to Professor Rosen's desire to deepen and broaden our understanding not only of Islamic law, but of law in general. The reader is inevitably led to wonder what a comparable examination of our own courts might reveal by way of underlying similarities. As with any original work, questions asked and answered raise yet further questions.

Alfred Harris, Editor
The Lewis Henry Morgan Lectures

Preface

It was Justice Holmes who once said: "If your subject is law, the roads are plain to anthropology." He might well have added, "or vice versa." For while neither law nor anthropology is coincident with or reducible to the other, the study of each may lack a critical dimension if considered alone. For the anthropologist, law – like ritual, politics, and marriage – constitutes a realm within which it is possible to see people acting in accordance with their deepest assumptions and beliefs; for the legal scholar, it is precisely in the concepts and relationships encountered in ordinary social life that many of the presumptions and procedures of the law find their predominant genesis and ultimate acceptability.

Yet despite their obvious points of coincidence, law and anthopology have not contributed as fully to one another as they might. Difficulties arise in terms of both subject matter and theory. As to the former, anthropologists have, with a few noteworthy exceptions, treated a predominant focus of the legal scholars – the operations of formal courts of law – either as a peculiar domain whose untypical language, rules, and procedures somehow remove it from the mainstream of cultural life or as an arcane realm that loses by its institutional rigidity the capacity to resolve disputes without alienating large segments of the population it serves. This avoidance of studying formal courts may be due, in part, to the tendency in our own society to view the courts as fraught with professionally skewed assumptions and far from disinterested goals, or to an outdated desire to show, contrary to colonial ideology, that native peoples possess law in every bit as refined a sense as do western societies. Similarly, legal scholars often approach the patterns of social and cultural life either as intrinsically interesting but not directly germane to the course of actual legal decisionmaking or in need of being kept distinct from law in order to establish or deny that the law may be reduced to explanations drawn exclusively in terms of economic, political, or psychological factors.

This mutual truncation of subject matter has its correlate in theoretical orientations. Anthropologists are frequently concerned to show that diverse features of social and cultural life have connections to one another, contribute to one another's operation, and move through time in relation to one another. Yet in the pursuit of elegant theories and the retention of the discipline's traditional focus on such topics as kinship, myth, and ritual, anthropologists for many years avoided those situations in which change, manipulation, and differential access to power might confute existing styles of explanation. From their side, legal scholars often sought to articulate the implicit propositions through which diverse judgments could be reconciled or to admit extrajudicial influences on the law only if those influences could be shown to form part of the conscious design or terms of discussion of the legal world itself.

The result of these topical and theoretical propensities has often been a sufficiently high degree of curiosity and fellow-feeling to allow nodding acquaintances to develop into episodes of mutual visitation where each discipline partakes of the other's exotic repast, tries on the other's peculiar garb, or is conducted through a quaint ritual of fictive kinship. But for contact to become conjuncture and itemized comparison to become integral concern it may be necessary to take quite seriously an approach that actually partakes of elements of both disciplines and which, by application across disciplinary lines, offers the promise of elaborating the insights developed by each. The approach in question suggests, quite simply, that the analysis of legal systems, like the analysis of social systems, requires at its base an understanding of the categories of meaning by which participants themselves comprehend their experience and orient themselves toward one another in their everyday lives. The institutions of class and money, power and privilege, far from being submerged by such an analysis, are seen to depend for their very impact on the broader system by which knowledge itself is produced; the significance of rules and procedures is seen to reside in their capacity to operate as systems whose constituent features are far more extensive and interrelated than our own disciplinary divisions may embrace. Seen in this fashion, law and anthropology are not just inextricably linked to one another; they actually constitute two sides of the same configuration.

It is from such an orientation, too, that an intriguing array of questions about legal and social life can be formulated. Instead of simply asking how judges decide cases, we can ask what some of the key concepts are that cut across the domains of law and culture giving shape to each. How, in the culture at large, are facts defined and truth conceived? How does the view of what persons are like take shape when the law must ask particular questions of character and state of mind? What role do cultural assumptions about the nature of human nature play in the development of evidentiary concepts, and how do these legally formulated concepts in turn evince themselves in the style by which people attribute actions to one another? To what complex of circumstances and relationships is the idea of power connected such that the law may address itself, successfully or not, to the general acceptance of its procedures and final decisions? By tacking back and forth across law and social life, by viewing both domains through a common frame of theory and practice, we can give serious consideration, in a way that may be applicable to a wide variety of societies, to the proposition that it is indeed possible to formulate a study of law as culture and culture as integral to law.

Few places offer greater opportunities for exploring the implications of these ideas than does the contemporary Islamic world. For westerners, Islamic law often incorporates images of a canonical system of medieval intricacy or criminal penalties of biblical intensity. In fact, for the one out of eight people on the planet who live subject to a legal system touched by Islamic precepts the role and importance of the law are inseparable from its connections to a wide range of social and cultural practices. By focusing on such questions as how the Islamic law judge exercises his discretion in a culturally characteristic fashion, or by questioning whether the forms of discerning facts and explaining causal links gain legitimacy in the law for being part of the common sense of a culture, it will be possible to explore, in ways that carry implications for western systems of law as well, how these two analytically distinguishable domains constitute a unified subject of study.

The chapters that form this book were first delivered as the 1985 Lewis Henry Morgan Lectures at the University of Rochester. Although the original format of the lectures has been retained, the text has been substantially revised and expanded. A series of notes and a still more extensive bibliography have also been added: they are intended to serve both as citations of actual sources and as guidance to the reader interested in the range of publications that have contributed to the present approach.

Like any author I am, of course, deeply indebted to many people for making this study possible. To Professor Alfred Harris and the Department of Anthropology at the University of Rochester I am extremely grateful for the opportunity afforded by these lectures and for the intellectual stimulation provided during my stay at the University. In Morocco, I am grateful to the Ministry of Justice, the Chief Judge and court personnel of the Sefrou District, and the many local officials who have made my work possible over the years. Colleagues too numerous to mention have given me the benefit of their thoughts, and I am especially cognizant of the tremendous debt I owe to Princeton University, Columbia Law School, the University of Pennsylvania Law School, Northwestern Law School, and the American Bar Foundation for the many opportunities they have afforded me. The typescript was completed during my tenure as a Visiting Fellow of Wolfson College, Oxford and the Centre for Socio-Legal Studies, and I am sincerely grateful to Donald Harris, Keith Hawkins, and Sir Raymond Hoffenberg for their hospitality. Funding for my work has been provided by the John Simon Guggenheim Foundation and the John D. and Catherine T. MacArthur Foundation, and I am most appreciative of the confidence they have reposed in me.

A special note of thanks must be addressed to my friend and colleague

Leonard V. Kaplan, who read the entire typescript with extraordinary care and insight and who, as on so many occasions in the past, has vastly extended the range of my understanding about law and life.

Finally, the book is dedicated to my wife, Mary Beth Rose, who not only shared with me an important part of the field experience, but has, through her deep appreciation of the human quest for meaning, contributed immeasurably to my own.

1

Law and culture:
the appeal to analogy

Several years ago I stood before a judge in an American courtroom nervously awaiting the outcome of a case upon which depended a great deal of my financial well-being and peace of mind. Together with my neighbors and representatives of several municipal and community organizations, we had – after the failure of many attempts at negotiation and political infighting – found ourselves with no other choice than to file suit against the public utility company whose practices were threatening to make the homes in which my neighbors and I had sunk so much of our fortunes and our energies both worthless and unliveable. As I stood there in that moment of inadvertent calm, when fear and diffidence are poised on the edge of another's decision, I could not help but reflect on several distinct impressions that had returned to me again and again over the course of the day's hearing. What a strange commentary it was on my legal education, I thought, that even though I was a lawyer, a member of the state and federal bars, and an adjunct professor at a nearby law school, I had, until this very moment, never once set foot in an American court of law! How ironic it was, too, I thought, that having spent innumerable hours in Islamic courts I was quite sure how best to argue the matter to a Muslim judge but far less certain of exactly what I should say in a court before which I was, in theory, actually trained to practice! So much was my experience of courtroom proceedings based on my Moroccan studies that I automatically began thinking in Arabic only to be struck by how odd it was that I could, without strain or hesitation, understand everyone – from the whispering clerk to the bailiff with the missing teeth – because every last one of them spoke my mother tongue.

But far and away the most striking impression I had in this entire process was the intense realization that here, in the lowest-level court of equity in the state, I was almost entirely at the mercy of a single judge - a man who, in his personal discretion, in an instant of seemingly boundless might, could magically lift or permanently affix a burden that had been laying upon me and my neighbors for almost an entire year. Like countless supplicants and cowards arraigned before an oracle, whether legal or religious, I tried to strike

1

a bargain with the spirits of the place. Earlier in the day I had shamelessly bound myself over to the position of the Legal Realists who had warned me to bend all my efforts not to an understanding of what the law on the matter is but to predicting what in fact the judge would do, and I was now ready to pledge myself, in return for a favorable result, to a life of mortifying realism and never-ending rule skepticism. Should circumstances demand, I was, however, no less prepared to barter my soul to the gods of Legal Positivism if only I could be assured that the judge, whatever the whisperings of his own moral sense, would realize that all of the valid legal rules were just as I had argued them and that the "uniquely correct decision" had my name written all over it.

But above and beyond all such promptings of legal artifice and craven servility I found myself repeatedly confronted by an overriding sense of fascination, a fascination which, I confess, was at that moment as much like that which a bird has for a snake as a scholar has for an enigma. For as impatient as I was to know *what* the judge was going to decide I was even more curious about *how* he was going to go about making his decision. So many things could sway him to one side or another, so many influences could be put together in different ways. Was it possible, I wondered, that he had had a fight with his wife at breakfast and would, in response, now leave me dangling from whatever legal peg lay readily to hand? Had he (I most devoutly prayed) himself once encountered a mean-spirited public utility official upon whom he might now avenge his ancient consumer's pride? Or was his line of thought, whatever its actual course, utterly beyond our ken – indeed, beyond his own – lodged in that murky brew of lawyer's art and psychic flaw out of which it is possible, as David Reisman once quipped about lawyers generally, to turn a personality defect into a professional advantage?

It was not, of course, only the ghosts of squeamish litigants and zealous counsel who shared with me their awe at just how judges do it. Justice Benjamin Cardozo, pondering the issue of judicial discretion, once answered the question, "What is it I do when I decide a case?" by posing a further set of questions:

> To what sources of information do I appeal for guidance? In what proportions do I permit them to contribute to the result? In what proportions ought they to contribute? If a precedent is applicable, how do I reach the rule that will make a precedent for the future? If I am seeking logical consistency, the symmetry of the legal structure, how far shall I seek it? At what point shall the quest be halted by some discrepant custom, by some consideration of the social welfare, by my own or the common standards of justice and morals? Into that strange compound which is brewed daily in the caldron of the courts, all these ingredients enter in varying proportions.

If, however, it is self-evident that a very wide range of factors goes into the exercise of judicial decision making it is no less obvious that, even where discretion appears most unbounded, it is likely to possess qualities that are at once distinctive to and characteristic of the time, the culture, the circumstances, and the background of those who exercise such judgment. Like so many other areas of nature and of human society, the problem is not in determining whether there are regularities to systems of law and aspects of judicial independence but how best to probe for and interpret these regularities. And as in so many other areas of common curiosity and scholarly investigation, we grope our way through areas initially uncharted and inchoate by applying to the unknown analogies drawn from familiar terrain. To understand how, as an anthropologist, I want in the course of this study to look at a particular legal system and the culture of which it is a part, it may prove helpful to see how the process of drawing analogies from one domain to the other and back again has in the past and may in the present case reveal features that might otherwise escape our notice.

It was Samuel Butler who once said that "though analogy is often misleading, it is the least misleading thing we have." Whether it is because, as Coleridge argued, an analogy partakes of the essence of the thing to which it is extended or because it is simply convenient for humans to approach the uncertain through such crabwise modes of thought, analogies clearly serve to direct or misdirect our inquiries and thus may speed or hinder access to an understanding of the thing itself. Surely it makes a difference to what we learn and how we move forward if we think of the eye as a beacon or as a receptor, the atom as a seamless sphere or as a miniature planetary system, society as a clockwork mechanism or as a living organism. One area in which the interchange of analogies from one field to another has clearly proved thought-provoking in the past has been in the nexus of law and anthropology. For some scholars this has meant extending the concept of rules, as prescriptive ordinances, as they are thought to exist in the law to realms of social activity – marriage, alliance, and network formation – not previously grasped in rule-like form. Others, working in the opposite direction, have sought to comprehend legal forms and legal change by drawing analogies based on the idea of physical and social evolution, the similarity of legal process to ritual activity, or the usefulness of reading legal sources like literary texts.

This study too will work back and forth, with the help of analogies, between law and anthropology, extending themes from each to the other. Specifically, I want to grapple with the problem of judicial discretion as a cultural phenomenon. And as might be expected from an anthropologist, I want to approach the broader aspects of this issue by cutting my teeth on the exotic – by trying to understand the nature of judicial discretion in the Islamic courts of Morocco. Since the Islamic judge, the *qadi*, has long been taken by western commentators as the archetype of the legal figure able to exercise vast discretion, there is particular appropriateness in taking these judges as our point of entry. But perhaps more to the point, if, as will be argued, a fuller understanding of judicial decision making can be gained by analyzing its cultural characteristics, it may be from the perspective of a distant culture that features of our own may be more clearly seen. The plan of this study, therefore, is quite simple: first to discuss, by means of a concrete analogy, an interpretation of Moroccan culture – a view of how some of the pieces of society, culture, and religion fit together in this part of the world and how, in broad outline, they manifest themselves in the proceedings I have observed that take place before the qadis. Then I want to consider how, in the context of this overall set of cultural assumptions and beliefs, the qadi faces the problem of determining the indeterminable – how he goes about discerning the facts in a case, indeed how he decides what shall be considered a fact, and how, drawing upon a style of reasoning that is both institutionally distinctive and culturally recognizable, he reasons his way to a final decision. If, as will be argued throughout, concepts of knowledge and right, of human nature and human utterance, play a central role in both the law and society of Morocco, then, next, it will be necessary to explore the implications of these concepts for the qadi by considering how he assesses what is in the public interest, how he and his culture calculate the consequences of individual acts, and how particular states of mind are attributed to individual actors. Finally, a number of these issues will be drawn together in order to formulate a specific interpretation of Islamic judicial discretion and the concept of justice that suffuses it. But no less importantly, it will be suggested that a cultural analysis of judicial discretion can contribute to the perennial debate on the nature of legal decision making and that such an approach may be helpful in the study of courtroom proceedings in western countries as well.

Like any scholar I begin from a baseline of certain assumptions, orientations that will influence both the choice of analogies and the overall goal. But scholars, unlike bankers, are under no obligation to make clear the price one is really going to have to pay for trafficking with them. Were we to legislate a sort of academic truth-in-lending, readers might be entitled to know at the very outset something of the overall orientation toward law and culture that will lie behind much of the present argument.

There have been many approaches by social scientists to the study of law, but I have not, I confess, been wholeheartedly attracted to any one of them taken in its entirety. I am not eager, like some, to demonstrate that *The Law* (spelled with capital letters and uttered in stentorian tones) evolves as a kind of driving force which an anthropomorphized *Society* nurtures in embryo in savage communities until, in the springtime of the species, it blossoms forth in a profusion of writs and deeds to challenge even the arts as the capstone of humanity's enviable achievements. Nor do I find myself taken with the idea that law is preeminently a mechanism of dispute *resolution* – an attitude which, even if one had never been involved in an endless and bitter legal case that never really resolved anything, could probably be dispelled by spending an afternoon in front of the television screen watching the sequence that runs from *Family Feud* through *The Edge of Night* to *The People's Court*, and back again. And while I admire their industry and erudition, I tend to regard those who have lost themselves deeply in the quest for an ultimate definition of the law as making even seekers after the Holy Grail appear the very embodiment of the Reality Principle.

Rather, it appears more fruitful to view law as part of the larger culture, a system which, for all its distinctive institutional history and forms, partakes of concepts that extend across many domains of social life. In law, as in politics and marriage, one has the opportunity to see ordinary assumptions put to the test of scope and implication, and though the response may be peculiar to its own domain, analyzing the realm of the law as a cultural phenomenon is no more unusual than viewing aspects of a society through the behavior of its members in the public market-place, the family dwelling, or the house of worship. Such a view of law is therefore indistinguishable from a view of how anthropological inquiry in general may be conducted – as a search for the concepts by which a community of human beings categorize and group their experience of an otherwise undifferentiated universe into packets of meaning, symbolically grasped and manipulated, as they go about arranging the relationships of everyday life. This is not, of course, to discount the connections – whether causative, dependent, or mutually supportive – that exist between law and its economic and political surround. It is, instead, to say that as people attempt to comprehend their circumstances and orient themselves toward them they grasp that world through categories and assumptions that are themselves cast up by the full range of historical factors that shape their lives. The anthropologist's task is to sort out these influences and to see how, given the particular issue under study, a balanced apportionment of the contributing factors best accounts for the matter at hand. In the analysis of contemporary Islamic law, it is necessary but not sufficient to understand the ways in which the struggle among contending interest groups and the tug of conflicting economic strains have enacted themselves in the forum of the law. For it is also necessary to see how the substantive and procedural ideas available at a given moment constitute the terms through which events are discussed, shaped, fought over, and fought for. The result, at any particular moment, may be one of simple imposition through existing institutions of the self-supporting concepts of the more powerful, or – as will be argued for the situation under study here – one in which a set of concepts, broadly shared throughout Moroccan society, suffuses a host of different aspects of collective life, thereby facilitating the struggle for individual success without the loss of a deeply felt collective order. And because the principles by which people can orient themselves toward the acts of others traverse analytically separable bounds of social life, it becomes imperative to see the legal realm – its struggles, its terms, its power, and its dependence – as an extremely characteristic part of the entire social fabric. It is from such an orientation – of conceptual ordering and institutionalized enactment – that one must try, often with the aid of metaphor and analogy, to understand the nature of judicial decision making and the constitutive role of law in Moroccan life.

During the course of many months stretching over nearly two decades, I have observed the proceedings and pored over the documents in the qadi's court of a city of 50,000 people called Sefrou which is located just south of Fez on the edge of the Middle Atlas Mountains. Lying between upland and plain, predominantly Arabic-speaking and largely Berber-speaking areas, Sefrou possesses many of the features and many of the strains distinctive to contemporary Moroccan life. Both the city and its hinterland have, through the course of many centuries, demonstrated in their organization, politics, and religious institutions their centrality and typicality of the nation as a whole. And while no single place can contain all variations that may be found in a complex society like that of Morocco, much less the entire Arab world, Sefrou embodies, in a theme-and-variation sense, an extraordinarily characteristic array of Muslim social and cultural features. It is, therefore, possible to enter the court of the qadi of Sefrou with the sense that, even in a single morning, one can gain a good appreciation of how a typical Islamic court operates and how judicial discretion is grounded in a cultural base.

The qadi's court is situated in one wing of the small palace built by a powerful administrator of the Sefrou region at the turn of the century. With its tiled courtyard and broken fountain, its shuffling clerks and toppling stacks of legal paperwork, the precincts suggest that mixture of Moorish ease and bureaucratic impulse that pervade so much of Moroccan official life. Although judges must be competent to sit in the civil or criminal proceedings that are the subject of other branches of the unified legal system, one judge continues to be designated as qadi, and it is he who enters the courtroom unceremoniously and, a clerk by his side, takes his seat at a table on a low platform at the front of the room. Those already seated in the court may continue to talk among themselves, return the nod of a passer-by viewed through the doorway that leads to the courtyard and lane beyond, or unflinchingly study the man at the front of the room. The qadi is a short, strongly built man in his early fifties, dressed in an ordinary jellaba over western trousers and sporting a bright red fez and a pair of tinted glasses. When he speaks, it is in a harsh, rasping voice which, however conversational its tone or abrupt its invocation, startles its listeners and commands their instant attention.

Litigants are called forward by a uniformed aide, a good-humoured Berber of the *ancien combatant* variety who not only tries to keep traffic moving and to translate for those few Berber tribesmen who do not speak Arabic very well but who, since the qadi's voice makes him difficult to understand at the best of times, repeats – often with embellishments and questions of his own – many of the qadi's utterances. As people come forward to be heard they may make some acknowledgment of the qadi – a curt bow of the head and shoulders by the women, a desultory military salute by the men – but the gesture is usually lost on the court or interrupted midway by the aide who nudges them into position before the qadi.

Regardless of the kind of case or the details contained in the petition and dossier on his desk, the qadi always begins by ascertaining who is who and how they are connected to each other. He is particularly careful to ask how people are related to one another when marital or inheritance matters are involved and to determine if the parties are speaking for themselves or through a spokesman. His first substantive question is usually the signal for the shouting to begin. Everyone wants to tell his or her side of the story, and no one seems eager to sit quietly while an opponent is speaking. Litigants and witnesses begin by talking to the qadi, but often end by addressing the aide, the clerk, the onlookers, and even a stray anthropologist. The qadi nods, listens, questions: the principals sit, stand, shout, and cry; the aide tries to quiet people by holding their hands down, in the certain knowledge that no Moroccan is comfortable speaking if he cannot gesticulate freely; and the clerk rushes to finish writing up the last case and find the correct dossier for the present one. Sometimes the qadi lets people shout at each other for a little while – whether to let them vent their anger or to gauge the intensity of their feelings – and sometimes he intercedes immediately to move things along. Eventually one person gets to tell a more or less coherent story, and women no less than men speak expressively and forthrightly with just that sort of keen timing and assured style they have developed in years of arguing before that most discriminating of judges, the crowd of relatives and neighbors who collect around any audible dispute. Most cases are handled with considerable rapidity: in the space of two hours it is not uncommon for the qadi to issue rulings on more than a dozen cases and to handle portions of a score of continuing matters. Often one of the principals will fail to show up or a necessary document will be missing, thus keeping a case from being heard in its entirety. Often, too, cases continue over a number of months and even years so that more than one qadi may have a hand in the matter.

The first case heard on this day involved a marital dispute. The wife stated in her petition that her husband forced her out of their home some three months earlier and had subsequently failed to provide her and their two small children with support. The qadi first inquired as to the area from which each party came and confirmed what the dossier listed, that they both came from a Berber-speaking settlement nearby in the countryside. In response to the qadi's questions the husband denied having forced his wife out of their home while the woman, in turn, acknowledged that she had neither witnesses nor notarized affidavits to support her claims. Without further inquiry the qadi ordered her to return immediately to the marital home and either offer proof of nonsupport in a subsequent hearing or risk having her case dismissed.

The next case, too, involved a marital dispute. Both husband and wife were from families whose members had, for countless generations, worked as craftsmen and gardeners in the city – a fact of which the qadi seemed to be well aware as he knowingly nodded his head while stating their personal and familial names. It was the woman's contention that the couple were living with the husband's family, that there were constant arguments between her and her in-laws, and that she wanted the qadi to order the husband to find them a new residence away from the husband's kinsmen. When the husband was called upon he spoke hesitantly, said it was all very shameful, and in a tone of familiarity and world-weariness allowed as to how the qadi must know that women are querulous by nature and that a new apartment would cost a lot of money. The wife interrupted to restate her claim in a way that indicated she knew full well the scope of her legal rights, to say nothing of the character of her in-laws. The qadi inquired as to whether other family members might help resolve the matter and whether more time might be useful, but the wife was quite insistent, and, after a moment's pause and in a voice fraught with resignation, the qadi ordered the husband to find the couple a new and separate place of residence.

Many of the cases heard by the qadi involve aspects of divorce, and it was as the result of one such divorce that the following dispute arose. The wife claimed that when the couple split up the husband kept a number of objects belonging to her, including some furnishings, tools, and clothing. Neither had witnesses who could appear for them. After barely a moment's inquiry the qadi ordered that the furnishings be given to the wife but that if the husband swore an oath that the clothes and tools were his, those objects would be awarded to him. If he refused the oath and his wife agreed to take it the items would be awarded to her. The husband said he would indeed swear the necessary oath before notaries at the mosque that Friday, and the matter was rapidly concluded.

The qadi also has the power to hear cases involving real property if any documents pertaining to it were initially drawn up by his court and if no title has been registered through a separate legal procedure overseen by a ministry and court in Fez. In a property case decided on this day the qadi was faced with a somewhat unusual situation. In constructing a new room on top of his house the defendant had placed a window in such a way that, the plaintiff claimed, it was possible for the women in his house to be seen by people looking out of the defendant's new window. The qadi had sent two of the experts attached to the court to determine the situation, and they reported back that it was indeed possible to see through the new window into the plaintiff's house, though one had to look at an angle to do so, a finding that raised the question whether the view was so intrusive as to warrant reconstruction. The qadi, refusing to hear any more testimony from the litigants and speaking more to the clerk than the parties, said that the school of Islamic law practiced in Morocco gives preference to positive assertions over negative ones, that the claim of actual harm is a positive assertion and should thus be favored over the claim of no harm, that people in the city as opposed to the countryside always place their windows so that one cannot see into another's house, and therefore that the defendant must indeed brick up his new window or move it to another place in the wall.

A small cluster of people now came forward in response to the aide's announcement of their case, and it took a little while before the jostling figures were sorted out and quieted so the qadi could proceed. He reminded himself who they were – he had, as a matter of fact, seen many of them quite often, since their dispute had been dragging on for more than a year. It began when the husband claimed that his wife left him and, though intermediaries of their tribal fraction had been sent to her father's house to request her return, she and her father had rebuffed all overtures at settlement. At the first hearing of the case the wife failed to appear and the qadi entered an order requiring her to return to her husband. Subsequently, however, the wife, with her father acting as her spokesman, appeared in court and said that the husband had actually divorced the wife several months before filing the present suit. A document was then produced in which two court notaries stated that fifty witnesses had appeared before them and attested to the fact that such a divorce had indeed taken place. The husband denied this claim and argued that the witnesses were not credible since they were all relatives of the wife and her father's family. The qadi then gave the husband the opportunity to request that a procedure be held whereby each of the fifty witnesses comes before two separate pairs of notaries who inscribe the testimony of each, and if the testimony of all remains consistent before both sets of notaries, a document will be presented to this effect to the court.

After numerous delays, in which both sides told the qadi they were having trouble getting all of the witnesses together, each party now appeared with a new set of documents. The wife presented a notarized assertion by twelve witnesses who stated that a divorce did indeed occur, while the husband brought an identical document in which his twelve witnesses attested to the exact opposite. There was considerable argument among the litigants and their respective cliques, but when the uniformed aide finally got everyone more or less quieted the qadi announced that whereas the husband's witnesses all came from the settlement in which the couple lived while those of the defendant-wife resided quite some distance away and would therefore be less likely to know about the couple's marital relation, it was the court's opinion that the wife should return to the husband's house and live there with him in peace. The prospects for this seemed rather uncertain as the collected relatives continued to shout and argue with great agitation while the aide jostled the entire lot out of the courtroom on the prow of his ample midsection.

By now the court had been sitting for several hours and the strain of hurried work, frequent bickering among the litigants, and the day's increasing heat were beginning to show. At times the qadi had clearly lost his patience, especially when delays led him to suspect, as he actually told some litigants, that they were just playing around with the law. He had listened quietly too, while some people told obvious lies, but if he regretted his inability to mete out punishment for such lying he never let on about it. Nor did he seem to mind that no elaborate deference had been shown to him as a high religious and legal figure or that the style of courtroom discourse appeared indistinguishable from that of a neighborhood dispute, a market-place squabble, or a family tiff. Eventually, with neither ceremony nor public acknowledgment, the qadi simply rose from his place and, with the dossier-laden clerk shambling after, walked briskly out of the courtroom.

In many respects the proceedings of the qadi's court are unlikely to strike western observers as particularly strange. Perhaps one might have expected greater formality, the occasional intonation of Quranic phrases, or frequent reference to obscure points of Islamic law. Although one might assume that the court has an essentially religious foundation it would be important to appreciate that its jurisdiction is nowadays limited to matters of family law and those property cases for which the court itself drew up the documents. The limited role it once played in the regulation of public morals – a role shared with the government appointed market regulator (*muhtassib*), the head of each occupational group (*amin*) and urban quarter (*muqqadem*), and various familial, residential, and religious intermediaries (sing., *wasīṭa*) – is, therefore, even further diminished at present. Contemporary Moroccan qadis must be competent to sit in the civil or criminal chambers of the unified court system and though specialization is usual, it may turn out that on an untypical day the "qadi" is actually a judge (*ḥakem*) from another chamber. Indeed, since it has been common in the Arab world since the earliest days of Islam for government officials to have their own separate jurisdiction, a number of issues touching on state policy and the well-being of the community of believers has never been within the exclusive control of the qadi. Perhaps, too, one might have expected women to speak less readily or less forcefully in their own behalf or to be less cognizant of their legal rights. Indeed, one might have expected in a tradition that pays such heed to the written word that even greater use would have been made of documentary evidence. But while the judge's rulings certainly do not appear wildly unpredictable or arbitrary, their precise rationale is not always self-evident. For even though the qadi is undoubtedly exercising his own judgment in some of the matters before him the real mystery lies in the particular way in which his engagement in such a process of discretion is shaped by the overall context of his court and his culture.

Why, for example, is he so concerned about people's social origins? What does such information tell him, and why is it relevant? When, in the first case of marital support, he asks few questions of the poor Berber country folk before him but tries to see if intermediaries might help resolve the claim of the urban Arab woman seeking a new residence away from her in-laws, is he using ethnicity as an index of interpersonal behavior or simply to sustain some prejudicial view of his own? Is he willing to grant the urban wife's request for a new apartment because of a clear legal right when, on other occasions, he has been known to dissuade a wife on economic grounds from pushing her claim? Or is he looking forward to a time when non-family members may be needed to witness the couple's conduct and the implementation of a court order? Why in the case of the divorced couple seeking a division of their property does he move so quickly to the use of oaths, rather than try to sort through the claims in a "more rational" fashion? Does the use of such an oath actually limit his discretion, and, if so, is that limitation affected by his decision as to which party has the opportunity to take the oath first and thus decisively end the case? What is the rationale, too, for the assumption, in the case of the wrongly placed window, that positive assertions take precedence over negative ones, and is the actual content of these assumptions decided by reference to classical Islamic sources or local custom? Indeed, how is such custom itself established: by the personal knowledge or beliefs of a qadi who in all likelihood comes from another part of the country, by what he is told is local custom – and by whom – or by experts who may not always agree? And if he is capable of scrutinizing with care the testimony of conflicting witnesses why should the legal system allow this capacity to inquire to be undercut when a litigant, like the man in the case of the questionable divorce, is simply able to obtain a document showing that his witnesses could keep their story straight before two separate pairs of notaries?

Looked at in this fashion, there appears to exist just below the surface of judicial decision making a host of assumptions, attitudes, beliefs, and modes of thought that call for closer inspection. These features, though clearly evident in the law, are not, however, distinctive to the realm of law alone. Indeed, it is precisely because most of the concepts and procedures employed in the legal system are replicated in a number of other domains of Moroccan life that the justice of the qadi reveals itself most clearly when seen in the context of the entire culture. In thinking about this particular instance of the relation of Islamic law and society it becomes useful, by way of analogy, to move back and forth across the various domains of social and cultural life in order to understand something about each of them.

The central analogy, the key metaphor, that may prove helpful when thinking about the social life of Morocco – and for that matter, of much of the Middle East – is concerned with notions of contract and negotiation. It is an image of the bazaar market-place writ large in social relations, of negotiated agreements extending from the realm of the public forum into those domains – of family, history, and cosmology – where they might not most immediately be expected to reside. For at the very center of Moroccan life stands not a set of corporate groups – tribe, family, or village – defined by collective endeavor or perduring structure, but the single individual who draws upon a set of regularized ways to enter into agreements with others and thereby construct a network of obligations as extensive and as fragile as his or her own negotiating capacities. It is as if, in the market-place of relations, one were able to operate in much the same way as in the economic market-place – arranging ties as advantage and circumstance allow and rearranging them, within the constraints of custom, law, and existing entanglements, whenever necessity, desire, and opportunity suggest their alteration. Just as there are societies in

Southeast Asia or the Pacific in which every activity must be the subject of ritual if it is to be at all meaningful to its members, or where, as in Japan or parts of South Asia, no act, from the mundane cultivation of the land to the terms by which people grasp their own identities, can be imagined that does not carry implications of hierarchical relationship, so too in North Africa there is a strong propulsion to envision and treat virtually every domain of life as subject to the capacity of human beings to shape that domain by the bargains they strike with one another over it. It is an orientation that tries to make sense of the world, and like any cultural system, it is itself comprised of categories and concepts whose distinctive qualities must be carefully unpacked.

The concepts involved in Moroccan views of self and society can be grouped into three main clusters: those relating to essential qualities of human nature, those describing the sources of one's social attachments, and those connected to the idea of mutual indebtedness and obligation. To Moroccans, as elsewhere in the Middle East, human nature is discussed by both men and women as a delicate interplay of reason and passion – ʿaqel and nafs. All individuals, it is said, possess both qualities, but the way in which they are weighted in particular kinds of individuals offers a clue as to the character and probable actions of those with whom one may arrange a bond – or those upon whom one may be called to pass judgment. Thus it is believed that while all individuals possess both reason and passion, the capacity for the development of reason is stronger in men while the impulse toward passion prevails in the nature of women. Children, it is said, are all nafs ("passion") and very little ʿaqel ("reason"), and for that reason it is necessary to channel their impulses by developing their reason through discipline, education, and proper attachments. Indeed, it is true throughout the life of any man or woman that prayer and affiliation with good leaders can lead to the prevalence of reason over passion, and it is, therefore, a matter of responsible choice to place oneself in those associations – with teachers, wise men, and enlightened authorities – through which one's own reasoning powers may develop. To understand and assess another's acts and character it is important to know something of his or her basic nature and the attachments that give it shape and definition.

Central to the conceptualization of these attachments is a second cluster of meanings revolving around the notion of asel. Asel translates not only as "origin," "patrimony," and "descent," but also as "authentic," "proper," and "strong in character." It thereby summarizes the idea that in one's social origins – in the people and geography from which one has drawn one's basic nurture – the traits and ties that an individual begins with can be most readily perceived. Where Americans might ask a stranger what occupation he practices, a Moroccan will ask about his "origins," his asel, the people and place from which he stems. Such an inquiry, like that about livelihood, gives the inquirer a key piece of information, for it suggests who this other is connected to and the ways in which he is used to forming such ties given the customs and practices of the region from which he comes. Like one's nature, one's *asel* – one's social identity – sets something of the parameters of negotiable relations and aids any assessment – whether personal or judicial – of those relationships.

The elements of human nature and social identity take on a more concretely contractual quality when set beside the third, and most important, of these Moroccan conceptual domains – the concept of *ḥaqq*. *Ḥaqq* means "right," "duty," "truth," and "reality." It is, in essence, a summation of the idea that all contacts between persons carry with them a sense of obligation – of something done and hence of something due in return. But although every act implies an obligation owed or a duty confirmed it is critical to note that the actual terms of such an obligation are themselves subject to constant negotiation and manipulation. Thus, if I help you in harvesting a crop you may try to build on the obligation that is implied by getting me to help you in forming a marital tie to one of my contacts or by supporting you in an election. *What* you may be able to get from me and *how* are deeply connected to your ability to play a set of such obligations in the way you see as personally most advantageous. And because it is this web of obligations that human beings create through their negotiated attachments to others that is the central feature of their existence, it is no wonder that *ḥaqq* should mean not only "duty," "claim," and "obligation" but "truth" and "reality." Indeed, because it is this obligational linkage that is so crucial to their concept of how reality is itself constructed it comes as no surprise to learn that attachments to Allah himself are viewed as contractual in nature and that He is the ultimate embodiment of this relational reality and is thus referred to, among his other names, as *al Ḥaqq*.

To deal effectively in the world Moroccans feel, therefore, that they must draw upon a repertoire of relational possibilities to construct a negotiated network of obligations. Aspects of a person's nature, origins, and web of indebtedness tell another how this person is connected to others, how they are most used to forming affiliations, and how they are most likely to act in differing situations. A constant quest for information thus ensues, a search for knowledge about the world and individuals' places within it. To know, for example, that another is a Berber from an area used to forming distant agricultural contacts and located at the center of a widely ramified series of such contacts is to suggest a host of specifics about how to deal with each other and predict one another's future acts. Knowledge is never without its practical implications, for the reason-governed person must seek knowledge of customs and relations in order to establish a zone of security in a human world where the rule of passions threatens the outbreak of societal chaos. This quest for information in a world of uncertainty is neatly summarized by a Muslim trader in one of Joseph Conrad's novels when he says: "In the variety of knowledge lies safety." And it is because Moroccans see the qualities of nature, identity, and network as themselves shifting from situation to situation that one can grasp a final concept of great significance, namely that of context.

The key word here in Arabic is *ḥal* – a richly varied concept from whose root is generated such meanings as "context," "situation," "weather," "state," and "condition." When, as they constantly do, Moroccans inquire of another's *ḥal* they are not just idiomatically asking about one's state of health or well-being but the condition or context within which the other was acting. For to know how another acts in a host of different contexts is central to knowing who another is, what he or she is most likely to do in other situations. Where, in the West, it might, at times, be assumed that an individual's personality can be given a basic definition that will manifest its distinctive features regardless of context or situation, Moroccans assume that it is context that makes visible character and that in order to know what another is like it is not enough to use terms and concepts that speak of a basic psychic structure; a description is also needed of what the other has been reliably reported to have said and done in a host of particular interactions. It is context that reveals persons, not the other way around.

What results, then, is a view of Moroccans as constantly engaged in bargaining out their relationships with one another, using as much information as they can to assess the way another is most likely to be attached to others and most likely to affect oneself. This negotiating process is true within the family – where the range of action is wide enough to allow detailed marital contracts, widely variant sibling relationships, and the need for overt agreements instead of reliance on generalized kinship obligation – and beyond the kin group, where solitary organizations are few and personally built networks of indebtedness are many. It is small wonder, in so personalistic a universe, that, as T. E. Lawrence put it generally, "Arabs believe in individuals, not institutions."

These general cultural themes manifest themselves in somewhat different but obviously related ways in a number of different domains of Moroccan life. Consider, for example, some of the distinctive features of Moroccan views of time and history. Since at least the period of the ancient Greeks people in the West have thought of time as having a distinct direction and shape. We speak of time as being like a line or an arrow; we envision it as marked by growth, development, and evolution. Such a vision of time couples with our conception of the individual and society as also growing and developing and of time and personal identity as linked to one another and mutually revealing. To Moroccans, however, individuals do not reveal the most essential feature of themselves – their situated networks of obligations to others – by means of a direction sustained over a course of time. Not only are such networks relatively fragile, but given each person's need to retain flexibility in a potentially chaotic world the moral, social, and legal universe is understandably ordered in such a way as to interfere to a minimal degree with the retention of this flexibility. Instead, time is seen as a series of discrete packets of experience, encapsulated instances in which the network of obligations characteristic of that moment are revealed. In Moroccan chronicles or accounts of ordinary occurrences, events are often related not in strict chronological order but as separate instances whose importance is not manifested by the temporal order in which they occurred. Each instance is instead a description of the ties that existed between the individuals involved at that moment; each is a description of a person in context. It would be as if, in trying to understand who another is, a host of photographs were scattered on a table showing that individual in a wide variety of situations. Where westerners might feel that an essential part of the answer to the questions, Who is this person? What is he or she like? would reside in arranging the photos in chronological sequence, Moroccans would focus on the issue of context – the way the person is reacting in each situated encounter. Time is therefore marked not as a line or even a cycle of occurrences but as encapsulated moments of interaction – what one Islamicist has called a "milky way of instants" – whose temporal ordering says far less about their participants' qualities than do the bonds of obligation they contain. It is as if, to use a different metaphor, each situated encounter showed another aspect, another facet of a distinct and variegated gem. To ask about a host of such contexts is to ask who another is: to fill in as many contexts as possible is to know as much as one can about how another acts under different circumstances and is most likely to act in the future.

The interpretation of Moroccan society that is suggested thus appears to have many similarities to western cultures, but in fact these similarities rest on quite different assumptions and carry quite different implications. In the west, as in the Arab world, great stress is laid on the individual. But where in the west this has come to imply the capacity of each person to fashion his or her own inner self and then to take that self and grant it a full range of political and religious support, in Arab culture the individual is the unit into which the features of background, context, and association are poured and through which the characteristic ways of forming ties to others are played out. Tribe, family, village, and quarter form an outer structure that provides the material that will cohere in the person, but not force any particular course upon him or her. This stress on the individual unit pervades numerous domains of Arab culture, from mathematics – with its emphasis on units linked into infinite chains – to architecture with its overarching designs that do not dictate internal elements but allow a series of discrete parts to be built up over the course of space and time. As one commentator has put it: "The stress on the individual part in Arabic literature, architecture, and music results in a loose, malleable overall frame or structure that has an organizing rather than a governing function. . . The concept of organization . . . emphasizes the individual unit and does not allow the open-ended and inconclusive overall framing structure to determine the nature or construction of a work's parts."

Similarly, in social life elements are constructed into chains of attachment within the framework of conventions that allow elaborate scope for individual effort. Everywhere the image of the contract reappears: in the bargain struck by God with prophets and with men; in ritual, where one may thrust upon the Almighty the need to reciprocate a duty performed; or in politics, where a sacrifice may oblige support or where coalitions may be couched in the terms of mutual aid in planting and harvesting. The features that take shape as individuals inscribe them through their personal efforts give clues as to another's likely moves and customary ways of forming ties. Thus, one can employ what might be called a code of cultural entailment that suggests that gender implies the force of passion versus reason, that the relation of passion and reason suggests how knowledgeable another may be, that knowledge implies one's relative social position, that position implies how extensive one's network may be, and that the scope and force of one's ties implies the extent to which one's acts have deepfelt consequences in the world. And because the framework of convention organizes rather than governs, each person must use language to great effect to build up networks.

From the perspective of the west, therefore, there is a tendency to think of the tremendous importance Arabs attach to the artful use of language as predominantly a matter of etiquette and rhetorical flourish. In fact, it makes more sense to realize that in this society language is the key instrument through which people negotiate relationships, and that, like a price mentioned in the bazaar, an utterance means nothing until a relationship is conceived in its terms. Thus the metaphor of bargaining and contract goes right into the heart of Arab social life, for the very terms that people use to conceptualize their relationships possess an essentially negotiable quality. Individuals can bargain over whether they will act towards one another mainly as cousins or as neighbors, whether an act shall be seen as an obligation or a favor, whether a situation is convertible to political aid or limited to financial expectations. And at each point it is the personification of features, not their abstract quality or the expectation of role behavior, that matters, whether in the reliance on personal testimony to the actions of another or the constant inquiry into another's set of affiliations.

The implications of this broad set of cultural categories and assumptions are enormous for every domain of Moroccan life, whether it be politics, religion, family relations, the structure of the market-place, or – to come round to the topic of this study – the realm of law and judicial discretion. For it is, in no small part, from these conceptual foundations that the nature, purpose, and quality of Islamic law and practice may be more fruitfully elaborated than by simple recourse to doctrine, statute, or opinion. If, as will be argued in more detail later, the central figure in Islamic law is not a corporate group but the legal person, capable of contracting his or her own obligations and thus inscribing himself or herself in a world whose quintessential reality is the arrangement of a network of *haqq* – of mutual indebtedness and obligation – it is against the background of the broader cultural concept of *ḥaqq* that these legal arrangements gain meaning. And if people may enter and exit such relationships with considerable freedom, it is essential that those mechanisms employed by the law to give shape and force to these relations be constructed in a fashion that conforms with, or at least does not fundamentally subvert, those common-sense ideas by which individuals continue to pursue the establishment of their own networks of obligation.

To look at the law, whatever its distinctive institutional features, as an aspect of culture, and to move back and forth analogically between these two realms suggests certain ideas that we will also want to explore in some detail. It is to suggest, first, that in a large number of instances, systems of law possess a very distinct form of indeterminacy. This does not simply mean that matters of substance or procedure may vary somewhat from case to case making simultaneous observation and prediction difficult if not impossible. Rather, it means that in most legal systems facts must be created as much as recognized and that the projection of such assessments on a screen of cultural, common-sense observations often creates a discrepancy, a lack of fit for which the authority and purpose of the law must seek to compensate. One sees this need for legal precision against a backdrop of conceptual inexactness in a host of different systems and instances. We may, for example, be called upon to adopt a legal fiction whose terms do not accord with the ambiguities of which we know the situation to be comprised yet accept it in order that a specific decision may be reached. Or we may state, with far greater certainty than is felt, that one or another parent is indeed the more fit to be given custody of their child in order that some clear direction may be given to the child's future. Though couched as statements of fact, legal decisions are, quite often, really creators of fact. Like religion, law is a kind of metasystem which creates order in a universe that is often experienced in a more disorderly way.

But where some legal systems have, for complex historical and political reasons, developed modes of conceptualization and styles of implementation that mimic the extrajudicial world rather little, in the Islamic courts of Morocco the metasystem of the law and the characteristic forms of its indeterminate judgments are remarkably close to the overall culture of its people. This is due in no small part to the goal of the law in this society. For rather than being aimed simply at the invocation of state or religious power, rather than being devoted mainly to the creation of a logically consistent body of legal doctrine, the aim of the qadi is to put people back in the position of being able to negotiate their own permissible relationships without predetermining just what the outcome of those negotiations ought to be. Whether it is in ordering a new apartment for a couple when the wife and her resident in-laws cannot get along or in their reliance on the role of reliable witnesses, the qadi's courts are devoted, in their procedures and their assumptions, to a goal that is deeply coupled to the course and concepts of everyday social bargaining. And it is the interdigitation of these legal and cultural factors that informs so much of the qadi's role and the exercise of his personal discretion.

There is a second aspect of Islamic law that flows from this as well. In the past, when western scholars have discussed Islamic law and the role of the qadi, they have generally remarked on the absence of doctrinal rigor and the presence of inordinate discretion. That is, they have characterized Islamic law – as opposed, say, to Anglo-American common law, European civil law, or Roman-Canon law – as lacking a rigorous set of logical links among the various aspects of the overall body of the law. Thus, it is noted that there exists in Islamic law no general concept of contract or tort around which judges and scholars could refine their conceptual categories as logic or concrete examples might demand. Coupled with this, in western eyes, is the presence of great and unguided discretion, for if the law lacks rigorous standards and principles the decision of the qadi seems to depend simply on his own feel for the equities or his own, perhaps prejudicial, opinions of the matter.

If, however, one looks at the actual course and goal of qadi decisions quite a different interpretation suggests itself – namely, that regularity lies not in the development of a body of doctrine which is consistent with other elements of that doctrinal corpus itself, but rather in the fit between the decisions of the Muslim judge and the cultural concepts and social relations to which they are inextricably tied. What judges in the system must therefore do if they are to accomplish the goal of setting litigants back on a course of negotiating their own relationships is to characterize those relationships at any given moment and implement their usual consequences by aligning their assessments with the characteristic assumptions that run through the course of life in its everyday enactment. That is why, as we shall see, everything from the style of inquiry and conversation in the court to the legal concepts of social utility and preferred approaches possesses a conceptual and a cultural consistency of quite a different nature than we, who look for legal and logical consistency, are most used to expecting. And that is why, too, what a qadi does and how he goes about doing it possesses attachments in the world that guide and channel his discretion in ways that are far from arbitrary and unbounded.

Indeed, it is these conclusions – about the particular nature of law as a metastructure with its own elements of indeterminacy and of judicial discretion as not being comprehensible without a clear understanding of the cultural concepts through which assessments of facts and consequences make sense – that must be given special attention. Such a cultural approach to judicial discretion also accounts for why, in later chapters, it will be necessary to explore the particular means by which Islamic judges determine the indeterminable and how they seek to comprehend the nature of a person's mind in a way that ties up with the assumptions prevalent in their culture. Such an exercise may also clarify why the qadi and his justice have been taken as the very antithesis of what is thought characteristic of western forms of justice. For it is the image of the qadi sitting in the corner of a mosque dispensing justice off the top of his head that has become, in Anglo-American legal literature, the archetype of the unprincipled judge, the man who, being dependent only on his own view of things, may decide as he pleases and thus engage in a process of adjudication fraught with the possibilities of political abuse. If, however, we look at his court as it actually operates and if we comprehend its larger cultural context we can see that it is a system with a logic and an order of its own.

Indeed, the qadi and his court may tell us something about us – even when it is, in a most inadvertent fashion, that we sense reverberations of his own style in a legal forum of our own. Perhaps that is why, when the judge before whom I so nervously stood in that American courtroom finally spoke, I felt I had come home again – to the court of the qadi of Sefrou. For rather than decide what it is the law says and therefore what the law demands, the judge allowed as to how he might just shut down an important part of the operation of the utility company if they, who had the expertise to find a solution, did not come up with an approach that would be perfectly acceptable to those of us who were being harmed by their operation. More of a qadi than a qadi, he set us on a course of negotiating a resolution to the problem ourselves. Perhaps, by way of recompense, we, too, can set off on a course that seeks to reduce neither difference to universals nor uncertainty to utter precision but rather tries, with the aid of analogies and our own interpretive powers, to glimpse a culture and a law that bespeak other ways of working through the conflicts of everyday life that seem at once so very exotic and yet so very human.

2

Determining the indeterminable

Whatever else a legal proceeding may be – an encounter between contending parties seeking confirmation of their respective claims, a carefully staged ritual aimed at the exorcism of potential chaos, a life-threatening confrontation with the manifest power of the state – it is not a simple recapitulation of a past occurrence. It is never really possible to reconstruct exactly the actions or utterances that gave rise to the case at hand: no witness can precisely recreate what was once said or heard, and even the videotape of an undisputed crime cannot delineate the inner state of the accused. Faced with such uncertainties any legal system must cope with the problem of defining as well as discovering facts. The system must not only seek ways in which personnel and procedures may be utilized for adjudication: it must also find ways in which, for purposes of authoritative decision making, a series of concepts and assumptions may be adopted or created by which an event may be designated as relevant or true. By deciding how to assess facts – indeed by deciding what shall be regarded as a fact – a legal system may create what shall be taken as so.

On its face the idea that courts create things as facts in order that they may be judicially recognized as facts sounds distinctly odd. But it is precisely the power of the law to make things so by declaring them so that is quite striking: when a judge says you are guilty, you *are* guilty regardless of any difficulties the judge may subsequently have in enforcing his decision or convincing others of its wisdom. So too when a court declares that a putative father is indeed a child's sire, that a promise is a binding obligation, or that an oath has conclusively established the truth. But where instances can undoubtedly be cited, in western law and Islam alike, of judicial fabrications proffered as obvious verities there always remains this curious relationship between the ability of the law to make things so by saying they are so and the evident need to perform this task in a way that remains broadly consonant with the sources of the judiciary's own legitimacy and the ordinary perceptions and assessments of facts that characterize the society of which the court is a part.

All of this is especially true of the system of Islamic law represented by the court of the qadi in Morocco. For as we have seen there is a high degree of consonance between the cultural assumptions and forms of negotiated social ties that characterize Moroccan society at large and the kinds of considerations to which the qadi must address himself in the implementation of the law and exercise of his personal discretion. Specifically, one must consider the ways in which the qadi goes about establishing the facts in a case, and the role played in his decisions by assumptions about the nature of language, truth, and the ways that human beings relate to one another. In the course of things it will be necessary to show how similar these legal concepts and devices are to those found in other domains of this Islamic society and to suggest why the legal and social realms may, in this particular instance, be so closely related.

In the preceding description of some of the cases that come before the qadi in a typical session it is important to realize that almost all of the evidence that the qadi received was oral in nature: physical evidence is rarely adduced in court and even documents seem to speak, as it were, less in the disembodied voice of a neutrally asserted fact than as the preserved tones of witnesses now absent or deceased. This might seem a strange quality for a society that is literate and that holds the written word in high regard. But it makes a good deal of sense if we broaden our view of courtroom evidence and procedure to understand in more detail some of the cultural assumptions that lie behind the Moroccan law of evidence. Far from being an obscure domain of technical detail, the field of evidence is, as Professor van Caenegem has said, "a field that . . . demonstrates the true position of the law in the general context of civilization: not as a marginal, abstruse technique of interest to specialists only, but part and parcel of the culture of any given period and one of its most important elements." This is clearly true of the law of evidence as represented in the relation between Moroccan culture and language on the one hand and, on the other, the nature of the proceedings that take place in the court of the qadi.

Moroccan society, it has been argued, is, like others in the Middle East, a highly personalistic society, one in which the single individual, as the fundamental social unit, draws on a series of relational concepts that gain further specificity as individuals create networks of interpersonal obligation. The words and deeds of men and women are the central resource out of which these webs of indebtedness are forged. Language thus becomes not just an instrument for expressing the preconceived or prearranged: it is one of the most critical resources by which one establishes one's ties, one's place, and one's self. Thus when disputes arise – when facts must be defined and assessed – it should come as no surprise that the legal system might turn to people's utterances to ascertain the nature and context of their differences. The only thing that is surprising, perhaps, is how thoroughly this emphasis on language as index and fabricator of the central facts suffuses the entire system of Islamic law and culture.

Take, for example, the crucial issues of witnesses. As the cases described so far indicate, the qadi is particularly intent on hearing the testimony of witnesses to the events in issue or receiving, through other court officials, indications of the witnesses' statements. In assessing the truth of their utterances, however, the qadi employs a set of cultural assumptions which have taken on a particular institutionalized quality in the law. These assumptions concern the perceived relationship between utterance and truth on the one hand and, on the other hand, the believability of the testimony and the character of the speaker.

Consider first the issue of truth. As previously indicated, Moroccans appear to make a clear distinction between statements made in the course of establishing a relationship and the truth or falseness that can be said to attach to any utterance. This distinction sounds peculiar to western ears since even if we do not believe someone who says he is our friend or who claims to know another person quite well we at least regard such statements as having some bearing on the issue of truth, as capable of being assessed at some level as true or false. But when a Moroccan makes such a bare statement, it is well understood that this utterance functions not like a statement that is true or false but rather like a price mentioned in the market-place, a figure that cannot be said to be true or false until it is accepted, validated by some additional act performed by oneself or another, and thus brought from the realm of the proposed into the world of activities that affect the relationships among people. Such a fractionation of utterances and truth makes a good deal of sense given the structure of Moroccan social arrangements, for it means that the things people say about relationships to one another really operate like bargaining positions and that a high degree of freedom is thereby afforded to arrange ties wherever they may prove most advantageous. Statements that work to create relationships simply are not held to standards of truth or falseness before they have been solidified by some act that brings them into the world of truth, the world of human relationships. Thus when one man says to another "You have an obligation to me" or "We are 'cousins' and here is what I'd like you to do for me," it is well understood that such a statement simply does not get assessed as true or false until, by some act of validation, the offer to define the tie in terms of kinship or proximity has been accepted. Only when this additional step occurs may one person seek to hold the other to the implications of their negotiated tie; only then does it become subject to evaluation as true or false.

Now the implications of this pattern of freely negotiated relationships that become transformed from offered bases of relationship into ties that can be held to their consequences are, for the law, profound. For the court must decide if a statement was just an unverified utterance, like a price mentioned in the bazaar, or a validated statement whose consequences the law must enforce. And, characteristically, Moroccan law has approached this evidentiary issue by trying to establish the stature of such statements before they actually come to the qadi and by assessing the truth of the statement by assessing the truthfulness of its utterer.

Since its earliest development Islamic culture and law have laid stress on the role of witnesses, who are believed to be able to attest reliably to the existence of certain facts. In religion, the authentic traditions (*ḥadīth*) of the Prophet's utterances and actions were traced through a chain of reliable narrators whose personal veracity served to authenticate what they had heard or seen. In law, this emphasis took on two forms: the use of the official notary, or '*adel* (pl. '*adul*), and the attribution of reliability, or '*adala*, to a witness. Both of these terms share a common linguistic root which means "to act justly," "to balance," "to set straight," "to equalize." Traditionally it was one of the primary tasks of the qadi to certify that a given individual did indeed possess the qualities of reliability so that his statements in court would possess a quality of truth about them. It was as if, by his demonstration in society at large of his willingness to stand by the implications of what he said, a man was holding himself out to the world as one whose statements go beyond mere articulation to become attached to the world of human consequences and hence of truthfulness. The emphasis on reliable witnesses thus recalls, in some of its functional implications, the use of legal fictions in other systems of law. For just as people may accept legal fictions as legitimate even when they know them to be false because such fictions produce results that are capable of being regarded as "true," so too, reliable oral testimony is, notwithstanding the tendency for people to forget or lie, accorded presumed credence in Islamic law because it is through speech that people achieve ties to one another that can be shaped to the preservation of a community of believers. When a person regarded as reliable by the court bears witness to a statement it is by the integration of his stature and his word that actions in the world may be transformed into facts that are at once judicially workable and culturally recognizable.

This personal quality of reliability was also early on institutionalized in the role of the professional witness, the notary. In Morocco, even in the present time, this institution takes the form of several pairs of notaries who officially witness statements made before them and reduce these utterances to writing in any of a variety of documents. Every marriage, for example, is, or at least should be, registered before two notaries, who record the terms of the wedding contract – the transfer of bridewealth, any payments that remain outstanding, and any conditions to which both parties have subscribed – and thus add their own believability to the statements and actions subscribed in their presence. Should a dispute subsequently arise, presentation of a document possessing the signature of two notaries constitutes a strong form of judicial proof. But note that this means that documents are really conceptualized not as reliable artifacts in their own right but as the reduction to writing of oral statements heard by two official witnesses.

It is not, however, simply for fear that documents may be altered that oral testimony carries greater weight. Rather, the legitimacy of the oral as the basis of knowledge rests, as we shall see, in no small part on the assumption that face-to-face interaction is necessary for the elaboration of those densely interwoven human ties by which social order is itself maintained, and the no less central proposition that the consensus necessary to that order can best be achieved when works and character can be assessed by those gathered in the speaker's presence. What notaries can do, therefore, is maintain, like a legal fiction, the image of oral authenticity even when the aura of direct observation is converted into a more indirect chain of reliable or professional relators.

People may not, however, have taken the precaution of having their relationships validated by notaries and must, when a dispute breaks out, seek a subsequent way of drawing their utterances into the realm of the believable. To be able to testify at all one formerly had to be certified as trustworthy in the first place, a process that involved calling others already so regarded to establish one's own character before the qadi. Such certification was at once a mark of a person's integration into the community and a matter which, in earlier times, was subject to enormous judicial discretion. Devices for certifying the reliability of a newcomer – from the use of local guarantors to judicial perceptions based on an elaborate "science" of physiognomy – were especially important in larger urban centers where not everyone could be personally known to the court. Yet it is equally important to see the practice of certifying the witness as the juridical version of converting mere utterances into truth-bearing assertions, a transformation that partakes of the deeper cultural scheme of allowing the free play of language to facilitate negotiation until it becomes so attached to the parties' acknowledged relationship that it acquires the social significance of a recognizable truth. Although the present court engages in no formal certification of reliability before testimony may be offered, it is clear that the qadi's assessment of a witness's statements continues to be influenced by knowing something of those features of background and attachment that formerly governed the certification process itself.

The emphasis on the direct oral testimony of witnesses is also evident in several other procedures used by the court. A party to litigation – or one who wishes to secure his position against possible litigation – may bring his witnesses before a pair of notaries who will certify that the statements were indeed made in their presence. While the notaries say nothing about the truth of what is being told them they do certify that the statements as recorded have actually been made. The number of witnesses appearing is also important. To present at least three witnesses is to acquire a document that the court will have to consider quite seriously; to introduce a document certifying that at least twelve people bear witness to an issue is to command still more attention. And to have each witness make his or her statement separately before two different pairs of notaries sitting apart from one another is to acquire a document of extremely persuasive quality. That an opponent may challenge one's witnesses or their statements, or present an even greater number of his or her own, simply underscores the emphasis found in court and society alike –

that statements must be weighed in terms of the known individuals among whom things have been said and actions observed.

The essential pattern, then, is quite clear. What we find in the law is a recognition of the free reign of utterance coupled with the need at some point to attach it to truth in a regularized way. The role of notaries as reliable witnesses for the court is not unlike analogous means by which ordinary utterances may be validated in social life. To make a statement valid people may swear by a particular saint or the Prophet that what they say is so, or they may commit themselves to some further actions in order to add validity to what was said. The process of testing for truth by quizzing numerous people to see if their stories are the same also has its corollary in non-legal settings. During the Middle East war in 1967, for example, many people asked me to listen to various European broadcasts, since consistency of the witness/broadcasts could be taken as proof of the truthfulness of what was being said. In the law the consideration of documents as redactions of the oral means that written formalities are of little importance, the key feature being whether the inscribed utterances stand up to the same sort of scrutiny to which one might subject the person actually making the statements they embody. It is, if you wish, a personalistic mentality carried over into a literate and complex legal system.

But witnesses, of course, appear in court no less than before notaries, and therefore the work of factual creation does not transpire alone outside the ambit of the courtroom. It is interesting to note, however, the way the qadi assesses oral testimony made before him. Earlier, it was suggested that in Morocco people are known by the contexts which describe their existence – the circumstances of their social origins, the qualities of learning or craft they possess, the range of situations through which facets of their interrelations and qualities have been arrayed and appraised. When, therefore, the qadi asks people about their backgrounds or circumstances he is trying to get a sense of who, by this society's criteria of identity, they are – what they have done or known or been surrounded by – for such information suggests to him, as to practitioners of everyday social intercourse, how another is accustomed to acting in various circumstances. To turn litigants loose to argue with each other is also to suggest just what the context of their dispute is. To scrutinize testimony is to apply social concepts of probity to legal constructions of fact. Thus, it is assumed that close relatives may lie on one's behalf and their testimony should, therefore, be screened out or clearly marked by the notaries when scrutinizing groups of witnesses appearing for a litigant. But it is also assumed that neighbors are more likely to know what is true about one's affairs than those living far away, and hence a limited series of co-residents are regarded as more believable than an even larger number of another party's witnesses who are not from his or her own locale. Indeed, as we saw in the case of the woman seeking a new place of residence away from her in-laws, Islamic law grants women the right to be situated, in the law's phrase, "among righteous people" because of the importance these neighbours may later play as witnesses to a couple's actions. And if a judge inquires into a range of other situations in which a person has been involved – matters that other legal systems might consider wholly irrelevant to the case at hand – it can be understood as an attempt to create a view of a man's character in order to create a vision of his likely actions in the matter under consideration.

Implicit in all of this is the notion that local circumstances and local attachments shape and define the people whom the qadi and his officials confront. If the court's means of drawing out the legally relevant suggests a tendency to force people's localized circumstances to speak for them, the use of other officials besides the qadi and the notaries suggests a similar effort to resolve factual issues by calling upon the assistance of people who will be most familiar with local circumstances. It is in this light that the crucial role of the court experts comes into play.

In a very wide variety of cases the disputants make assertions of fact that contradict one another or seek monetary awards the court must assess. One of the primary devices the court employs in these situations is the use of experts appointed and paid by the court. There are usually two experts who specialize on each of several substantive topics – property boundaries, marital and child support, and issues involving the construction of buildings – as well as one woman who is knowledgeable about matters relating to women's bodies. The experts may be asked to apply their knowledge of the locale and circumstances of the parties to establish, for example, the amount of money people of the litigants' background can normally be expected to need for housing, clothing, or food, or to guide the court by attesting to the quality of materials normally used in buildings of a certain type and location. There are, it should be noted, two culturally characteristic features that are especially important about this use of experts.

First, we have the use, as is also the case with the notaries, of people who have the sort of firsthand knowledge the court itself may lack. Moreover, these functionaries are used to prepare and clarify otherwise disputable information for consideration by the court. When the court uses their findings it thus not only distributes some of the burden of its decision to those who are deeply involved as respected and knowledgeable members of the market-place; it also makes the choice of a given award appear less arbitrary for being based on the shared opinion of several others. It is yet another indication of how the legitimacy of the law rests not on some simple religious or political base but on the concept of personalized knowledge and reputation which is the driving force of ordinary Moroccan quests for information and affiliation.

But the experts also do something else – they draw customary practice within the ambit of the law. For the source to which they turn for information and standards is one that is neither artificial and legal nor personal and discretionary: it is the practice of people in the area as known and articulated, in particular, by those who have dealt with such matters so regularly and so

well that people in the market-place have come to refer to them as masters
(sing. *m'alem*) of their trade. As we will see later, this personally authenticated
knowledge of local practice has its correlative manifestation in the mode of
judicial reasoning itself. Here, the central point to appreciate is that once again
the way evidence is sought and shaped is, as the use of the experts exemplifies,
one that pushes fact-finding down and away from the qadi so that when it does
arise for his consideration it is less his arbitrary decision or an abstract rule of
law that seems to apply than the standards – often quite variable across
regions – of the particular locale of this court. Such an emphasis is, moreover,
legitimized by strict Islamic law, which sets substantive standards on relatively
few practices, leaving within what the Quran repeatedly calls 'The Limits of
God' considerable scope for the varied practices of humanity. And this
religious legitimacy is, in turn, supplemented by the common practice of
people in the region – a practice, as always, that gets much of its own regularity
from its acceptance by those regarded as knowing most about it from their
own experience and success.

Moreover, court experts, like legal presumptions, also serve to sort out
physical evidence that might be relevant to a case, whether it be in deciphering
the existence of a contested passageway from the architectural traces left from
before its closure or the establishment of the injuries inflicted on a wife by the
husband she is suing for divorce. Direct physical evidence – the existence of a
newly built structure or the presence of another on disputed land – is readily
introduced and acknowledged, particularly when brought to the court's
attention by the experts. Where some inference is necessary it is interesting to
note that the court tends not so much to weigh the evidence against absolute
"scientific" standards as to treat it as confirmation and elaboration of the
local testimony or character of the parties. Even those legal presumptions
against which evidence may be measured tend, as we shall see, to be couched
largely in terms of human nature and relationships. These qualities are readily
discernible in what is often taken as the archetypal instance of circumstantial
proof, namely the Quranic version of the story of Joseph and Potiphar's wife.
In the Old Testament, it will be recalled, when Joseph refused the woman's
overtures she snatched his cloak and claimed Joseph had dropped it when
trying to assault her, a claim that landed Joseph in jail, where he began a new
career interpreting dreams. In the Quranic version, Potiphar's wife makes a
similar accusation after Joseph spurns her. But in this account one of the
woman's own kinsmen points out that the garment is torn from behind, not in
front, proving that it had been grabbed as Joseph was running away from
Potiphar's wife and not, as she testified, when she was fending off his attack.
Although cited by some Islamic judges as support for the admissibility of
circumstantial evidence, the Quran itself does not make this argument. Rather
it draws from this story the lesson that women are by disposition perfidious
creatures and that even their own kinsmen should beware of their guile.

In most circumstances, then, it is oral testimony and character assessment that constitute the basis for the qadi's inquiry, not because inferences from physical evidence are unknown but because the court has developed far more elaborate techniques for dealing with the whole process of witnessing than for evaluating circumstantial evidence. The confidence both the court and its clientele place in oral testimony is perhaps related to the criteria used to assess consequences and harm – the effects of occurrences on people's relationships – whereas the development of techniques to discern physical evidence might be less compatible with this overall orientation. Where in the west we have increasingly de-emphasized the personal attributes and background of litigants and defendants and sought to refine our legal and technical evaluation of physical evidence, Islamic courts continue to stress the person rather than the single event and thus feel more comfortable with oral than with material testimony.

The basic modes of shaping facts for the qadi – the use of reliable witnesses, experts, and forms of judicial inquiry – are, of course, adequate for the normal run of cases, and though their implementation is never simply mechanical the routine of judicial institutions removes from many cases the need to confront contradictions that may arise between and among the various sorts of proof that may be offered. It is when such conflicts arise, however, that we have a chance to test the scope and implications of the different standards and institutions involved.

The qadi may, in certain instances, be called upon to decide on the credibility of conflicting proofs. It is not unusual, for example, for both sides in a dispute to present notarized testimony by opposing sets of witnesses and for the qadi to probe for the greater believability of one set over the other. Initially he may assess the evidence in terms of a series of assumptions that have become judicially regularized. He will, for example, regard those who live nearby as more likely than those who live farther away to know if a husband has indeed been mistreating his wife, to give the subsequent testimony of witnesses to a land transaction less weight than a notarized document made out at the time, or to regard as more credible those who claim actually to have seen a marriage celebration take place than those who simply heard about the event. Cultural assumptions, molded and articulated by judicial action, deeply suffuse the content and application of the court's assessment of facts. Indeed what is particularly striking in this system is the similarity of the concepts by which courts and ordinary people think about human nature and interaction, and how few are the juridical rules or procedures that differ sharply from those employed in numerous other domains of the community's life. Whether it is in the scrutiny of individual's statements or the evaluation of a couple's marital discord, the mode by which the court sorts out the credible from the doubtful is remarkably lacking in institutionalized distinctiveness, notwithstanding the highly developed nature of Islamic law.

On rare occasions, however, it is the very presumptions with which the court operates that have been confronted by alternatives. This appears to have occurred, in recent times, mainly as the result of colonial intrusion or the adoption by the newly independent state of procedures derived from European examples. Where such conflicts of presumption have become evident they are intriguing both for the differences they pose and for the characteristic qualities of the larger culture they reveal. Take, for example, the problem that may arise when conflicting assumptions have become institutionalized in the procedures of courts with overlapping jurisdictions. A case brought by an elderly informant during the course of my first field trip in the mid 1960s will illustrate the problem.

Haj Hamed owned a house in one of the old quarters of the city of Sefrou. Like most such houses it shares its outer walls in common with its neighbors'. Many years ago the Haj wanted to add a new room on the top of his house, the outer wall of which would form a party wall with his neighbor. Since the Haj's neighbor might be able to make use of the new wall for a later addition of his own it was, and indeed is, common practice for the neighbor in such a situation to contribute to the cost of the common wall. But the Haj's neighbor refused to pay his share. It was here that the Haj made his mistake. What he should have done was go to the qadi's court, preferably with some witnesses and even better with the neighbor himself, and have the notaries prepare a document in which the Haj and others would testify that no money was ever received from the neighbor for the new wall. But the Haj never bothered: he simply went ahead and built his rooftop addition. Now, almost forty years later, the Haj's neighbor set about adding a room of his own on the roof and the Haj, who is not the sort of man to let such matters pass unnoticed, figured he finally had a chance to collect his due. But he had a problem: to make his case to the qadi he needed either the notaries' document or witnesses to the original event, and the Haj could not produce either one at this late date. However, he did have an alternative available. Since Independence the Moroccan government had reorganized the judicial system leaving to the qadi's court jurisdiction over matters of personal status – basically family law and inheritance – and those property matters for which notarized documents could be presented in evidence. In addition they established as a separate wing of the judicial system another court that handled criminal and administrative cases – and those property or personal injury cases for which no notarized documents existed. Although the latter court has no notaries attached to it it does employ various experts. And because the law did not establish a clear jurisdictional line between the two courts on types of cases or amount in controversy the Haj could, in effect, choose his forum on the basis of his available evidence.

More importantly, the two courts make precisely contrary presumptions in their application of the relevant evidence. The qadi's court presumes that if one has a notarized document saying the neighbor never paid his customary share that position represents the truth unless a contrary form of witness proof is offered. However, if neither side has any documents or witnesses it is presumed that the neighbor must have paid his customary share – else why did the builder of the wall not get a document attesting to the contrary? – and the defendant will automatically prevail. But the new court makes the exact opposite presumption. If the experts report back that a neighbor is indeed using a party wall, this other court presumes the neighbor has *not* contributed to its construction unless the neighbor can prove he has. So even though the Haj cared little for a court that did not rely on the tradition of the notaries, he was only too willing to get even with his neighbor by availing himself of the alternative presumption applied by the newer court.

This case thus provides a striking example of conflicting evidentiary standards, judicial change, and the relation of law to custom. Leaving aside for the moment the relation between cultural concepts and legal presumptions – the shift, in this instance, that has occurred in what I will call the calculus of consequence – it is clear that the case of the party wall suggests a conflict in the way these two courts create facts. The qadi's court creates facts primarily through the medium of oral testimony substantiated and validated by reliable witnesses in the form of the notaries or adequate numbers of credible witnesses, and secondarily by the use of experts. The new court is no less eager to hear and scrutinize actual testimony, but it is more ready to substantiate experts where actual testimony is lacking. Both share the tendency to leave fact-finding to persons other than the judge, but because they calculate consequences differently a genuine difference in factual creation has come into existence.

A more common example of the conflict of presumptions arises in those cases in which western scientific propositions conflict with traditional beliefs. Medical evidence in particular creates distinct problems for the court. Islamic law has long accepted the idea, for example, that a woman could be pregnant for much longer than nine months, a rule that may have served well when travel was lengthy and legitimate heirship preeminent, but which clearly contradicts modern science. Or medical testimony concerning an injury done to a woman by the alleged sexual mistreatment of her husband may contradict the conclusions offered to the court by the woman expert sent to examine the wife. Some but not all of these contradictions have been resolved by the Code of Personal Status which, to cite just one example, fixes the maximum period of pregnancy at one year and allows both doctors and the court to be involved in determinations up to that limit.

The acceptability of scientific versus indigenous concepts may test the attitude of the court no less than the legitimacy of its methods. Throughout, two impressions remain uppermost. First, that whenever possible qadis try to obtain information *both* from outside experts and their own, using to the maximum their modern statutory grant to appoint any kind of expert and their right, acknowledged by the highest court in the country, to ignore what the experts say provided that the court gives clear reasons for doing so. By using multiple experts the qadi, characteristically, draws upon local knowledge and spreads the risk of formulating an unacceptable result. But no less importantly, the qadi, secondly, shows no hesitation in letting extra-judicial expertise be as much a function of his reading of the total circumstances of the case and the character of the parties involved as of the factual nature of the problem presented. Thus where medical data may be sought when contending parties have no greater attachment to one another than the circumstances of the present case or where, for whatever reason, the qadi is not interested in exploring their interlocking ties, he may be willing to use modern medical testimony because the case does not call for the continuation of relationships toward which traditional procedures are more oriented. In both cases, the qadi's focus on consequence rather than abstract rules offers characteristic support to his method and the acceptability of its results.

Problems of factual determination may also arise, of course, if the two experts assigned by the qadi – or, for that matter, the 'civil' court – disagree with one another. Although no instance of such a case has been encountered in the records or memory of the court in Sefrou, both the published opinions from other jurisdictions and the remarks of interviewed qadis conform to a single approach, namely, that the judge must decide between experts who disagree using as his guideline a principle we have already encountered – that the party who claims he or she is being injured should be favored over the one who denies that harm is occurring. Such a principle not only shifts the grounds of consideration from that of absolute to relative concerns but clearly allows the decision to be made on the basis of maintaining the status quo. And since it is widely acknowledged that custom is habit and habit expresses the general accord reached in society, the court tends, not surprisingly, to create as fact what has already been established de facto in society. When the court does reach out for change, as will be seen later, it often does so in a fashion that is characteristic of this society, by attaching their decision to the changed practices in the community or the opinion of one whose reputation has grown to great proportions.

If it is true that courts cannot recapitulate events but can only "construct" them, then it is also true that situations may arise where opposing assertions are equally weighted and no one can say, without invoking either a legal fiction or a presumption, what is really the truth. Faced with such a situation the court of the qadi utilizes a mechanism which is not unusual in comparative legal history – the decisory oath – a mechanism which, in its invocation and in the manner of its application, is nevertheless characteristic of many aspects of Moroccan culture.

Taken from the perspective of contemporary western jurisprudence the oath is usually regarded as a quaint ritual by which we try to conduce witnesses to be truthful, as a procedural basis for punishing liars for perjury, or simply as a relic left over from a time when, in the absence of more rational fact-finding mechanisms, indeterminable issues were submitted to divine adjudication. A century ago, a justice of the Ohio Supreme Court neatly stated the modern rationale for the oath when he remarked:

> The purpose of the oath is not to call the attention of God to the witness, but the attention of the witness to God; not to call upon [the Almighty] to punish the false-swearer, but on the witness to remember that [God] will surely do so. By thus laying hold of the conscience of the witness and appealing to his sense of accountability, law best insures the utterance of truth.

It is not, however, to the use of the oath as an admonition to the witness that Islamic law has recourse to this device. Indeed, witnesses are not sworn before testifying, even in criminal proceedings, nor is any punishment for perjury recognized – the common assumption being that in the face of such proceedings one may well be expected to make statements that do not bear on the truth. Rather, the oath is predominantly a mechanism for the establishment of judicially cognizable facts, and as such the assumptions and procedures it incorporates partake deeply of concepts and approaches found in other domains of Moroccan life. In a society in which, as we have already seen, it is well understood that people must be free to make statements that could bring relationships into existence without truth being an immediate consideration, so, too, in the legal realm this common practice is recognized and witnesses are allowed to speak freely and judges to inquire cleverly, and no one is held to the implications of truth until truth is made to attach either by a final oath or by an official pronouncement of the court. Oaths, in law, thus fix what has been said, bringing it into the realm of the true, just as acceptance of a price in the market is the act that makes the price count as true for the relationship formed through it. And just as there are conventions for the way an utterance in social bargaining takes on aspects of truth, so, too, the law possesses, through the oath, a mechanism for affixing the articulated as true.

Oaths may take several different forms in Islamic law. We have in a sense already seen one version of an oath in the group of witnesses who come before one or two pairs of notaries to have their statements attested by reliable court witnesses. This form of collective oath-taking may have received impetus in Morocco from the Berber custom of co-swearers, a process which, like the oath of compurgation in medieval western law, involves a group of men who collectively offer their testimony. Among the Berbers, the usual process was for the plaintiff to choose the defendant's lead witness and for the latter to choose an additional forty men to join him in the oath. As in the compurgation oath in the west the swearers were attesting not so much to the facts in the case as to the character of the defendant. In effect what the lead oath-taker states is that "I, a man you the plaintiff have chosen for his reliability, assert that the accused is not the sort of man to have done what is charged and I have gathered these others who will back me in making this statement of his character." In this situation, to paraphrase Aeschylus, perhaps it is not the oath that makes the man believable, but the man the oath. The use of group witnessing in the qadi's court, however, is directed toward the question of actual occurrences rather than character, and the court will subject even the testimony sworn separately before two sets of notaries to rational scrutiny.

The testimony of litigants and witnesses, as well as the notarized documents they introduce, may, of course, be totally contradictory. Or there may simply be no evidence on either side to support the various contentions. Short of invoking a legal fiction or presumption the court may be asked by one of the parties – or may itself require of one who hopes to further his claim – that a holy oath be sworn in support of the litigants' assertions. This decisory oath is a key ingredient in the shaping of the qadi's justice and discretionary powers.

On its face the procedure appears rather mechanical. If neither side can present adequate support for its claim one party may challenge his opponent to take an oath in support of the latter's assertions. If the opponent does so he automatically wins the case. If he chooses, however, he may refer the oath back to the challenger, who may conclude his victory by swearing to his claim. This system is by no means unique to Islamic law. Indeed, it is still possible in Spain, Holland, France, and Italy for one litigant to demand that the other take the oath or refer it back to him, the first to swear being the winner of the case. What is unusual about the Islamic system of decisory oaths is that it is up to the qadi to decide which of the two parties shall, for the purposes of taking the oath, be designated as the one who may first challenge his adversary to take the oath. Since the first to swear cuts off the other entirely the designation is crucial to the outcome. But where, in other systems of law, the priority of oath-taking is determined simply by who is the plaintiff or defendant in the case, in Islamic law the court may designate either party as the one who may issue the challenge first. The qadi's decision thus infuses the decisory oath with a number of rational and cultural elements that take it far beyond a simple matter of rational proof or arbitrary discretion.

Indeed, it is possible to characterize the process by which oath-taking is allocated with some specificity. The basic source for this procedure is said to be the assertion by the Prophet Muhammad that "the burden of proof is on the *mudda'i*; an oath is incumbent on him who denies." This term *mudda'i*, and its opposite *mudda'a 'alay-hi*, have been characterized by some as, respectively, the plaintiff and the defendant, or as the one who says "it was" versus the one who says "it was not." But this does not accurately fit the cases. A complex, but more accurate definition, by an early commentator, states; "the *mudda'i* is he whose averment lacks both any ordinary and any special presumption in favor of its truth; and the *mudda'a 'alay-hi* is he whose averment is supported by one or another of those presumptions." In other words, the qadi looks for the person who is presumed most likely to know what is true about the matter at hand or the one who is presumed to have been carrying out his or her tasks correctly, and he then designates that person, whether he or she instituted the claim or was the one sued, as the person who might first be challenged to take the oath. Several examples may help to clarify this point.

In Moroccan law, both before Independence in 1956 and since, it is the mother and her relatives who are, in the event of a divorce, accorded custody of a child until the child reaches maturity. To retain charge of a child the custodian must possess certain qualities, described in the present code as reason, maturity, honesty, the ability to raise and protect a child, and the absence of any contagious disease or relevant disability. But when, for example, a father sues for a change of custody because of the existence of some impediment in one of these qualities it makes all the difference whether the law presumes that the present custodian does indeed possess these capacities or requires her to prove that she does. In most cases it is in fact the defendant, favored by the presumption that he or she is entitled to remain undisturbed, who by taking an oath can cut off any further recourse by the plaintiff. If, however, a dispute arises in which the court believes that, in the normal course of things, it is the plaintiff who has the greatest degree of knowledge of the relevant issues it is that person who will be designated as the "defendant" for oath-taking purposes. Thus, as we have seen, the court will require a husband to swear that objects that would normally belong to a man are indeed his even though it may be he who initiated the suit for a division of marital property. In the child custody case, the approach generally accepted by Moroccan courts is that the person who actually has custody is presumed to possess the qualities of a custodial parent, and the person who denies that the custodian has these qualities is designated as the "plaintiff" for the purposes of the oath. This means that all other avenues of proof having been exhausted, the custodian need only swear that she meets the stated requirements and she will have established her claim to continued custody. Were the presumption reversed – as some commentators argue it should be – the matter might more likely be resolved in favor of the challenger. As always, the party who first has the opportunity to take the oath may refuse to do so, thus affording the opponent the chance to win the case decisively by swearing to the truth of his or her claim.

Now there are a series of fascinating issues raised by the use of oaths in these legal proceedings. One that may immediately come to mind, of course, is that it affords liars a fairly easy opportunity to win their cases if they can simply get themselves designated as defendant in a suit of their own creation. It is important to appreciate, however, that at least in the past, the sanctioning power of an oath was very significant. Many people to this day strongly believe that a false oath will definitely incur supernatural sanction, if not immediately then in the long run. I have myself not only seen many cases where one person refers the oath back to another: I have even witnessed a case in which a person maintained his claim all the way from the court to the mosque where the oath was to be taken only to stop on the doorstep, refuse to swear, and thus relinquish his preemptory right to conclude his claim successfully. The fact that the outcome of a case cannot, on the majority view, be overturned even if a person is subsequently shown to have sworn falsely further demonstrates the importance that the courts, in the traditional absence of an appellate structure, attached to achieving finality. Perhaps, too, notwithstanding modern appeals courts, the qadi is well aware that if his "final" decision simply provokes further disputes he will very likely have the chance to rehear the parties at some future date.

But there is doubtless another aspect to the use of decisory oaths, namely, that people often know, or think they know, the true facts in a case, and if they see another is willing to swear falsely they are less likely in the future to want to form a negotiated bond with such an unreliable person. Thus, once again, the personalism of Moroccan social relations, the need and ability to forge ties wherever they prove most effective, can contribute to an individual's unwillingness to risk his overall attractiveness as a partner in favor of a short-term gain others believe has been bought at the price of a false oath. And because the oath is, in extrajudicial contexts, one of the primary vehicles through which ordinary utterances are brought into the realm of the truth – the realm of human relations – there is even further support to the maintenance of this legal mechanism whatever the range of contemporary theological assumptions.

Clearly, then, the oath is far from being an irrational mode of fact-finding. For quite aside from the mundane sanction that may attach to its violation it is clear that in legal cases the oath is preceded by a highly rational process of assignment – to a parent already having custody, to a man concerning what normally belongs to a man, to a bride claiming to have been a virgin – all of which are based on reasonable cultural assumptions about the nature of facts, human relationships, and desirable social consequences. Indeed, instances like these suggest that there may be a very strong rational element in the use of oaths and even ordeals in various legal systems, but that the rationality lies not in some psychological or scientific proposition that the people involved have not adequately articulated – that lying increases the heart rate, which makes the administered poison of an ordeal work, or that one who believes he is telling the truth can psychically keep his hand from burning when it is immersed in a vat of boiling liquid. Rather, such oaths and ordeals may tend to be assigned to those whom society has reason to believe are most likely to know the truth, and by leaving them a way out – by referring the oath back to another, in the Moroccan case – both that assumption and the social relations the use of oaths tends to uphold are given effect and consonance with the idea of a divine justice that informs an Islamic community of believers.

Indeed, it is this last point – of the order and coherence that the court of the qadi seeks to express and maintain – that can help us to understand the use of oaths in particular and some of the central qualities of Islamic legal systems in general. Oaths, as we have seen, can be said to possess both rational and irrational features, and indeed it is in these terms that most legal theorists, usually following the typology of Max Weber, have discussed them. These discussions naturally recall, for anthropologists, those that have gone on for more than a century about the nature of magic. For just as E. B. Tylor and Sir

James G. Frazer could argue that the practice of magic by primitives was a distinct, if misguided, attempt to conduce a world of natural occurrences to conform to human explanations or acts, so, too, oaths could be regarded as invoking a sort of prescientific science to bring the indeterminate into accord with a human need to comprehend and constrain. And just as Bronislaw Malinowski could argue that magic functions to support the individual's psychological need for certainty and orderliness and is, therefore, called into use only when that need cannot be fully met by acts that obviously produce desired results in the everyday world, so, too, one can easily find in the use of oaths an attempt to resolve disputed facts which common sense, cultural assumptions, and judicial scrutiny cannot adequately establish. But the problems inherent in such analyses of magic are equally prevalent when oaths are considered – of reifying individual psychology on the basis of collective acts or assuming that beliefs can be categorized as correct or mistaken, rational or not.

In recent decades students of magic, ritual, and religion have, however, broken away from these earlier dichotomies and have come to suggest that these practices are more fruitfully seen as expressive events, acts by which the members of a community draw on the store of symbols through which they have publicly inscribed their assumptions and beliefs and displayed to themselves a vision of the world that, for them, makes sense. Such a perspective avoids the constant attempt to draw distinctions between the magical and the scientific, the rational and the irrational – as well as sterile debates over who has more of which, them or us. Instead, it puts the focus on the coherence or lack of coherence of a society's assumptions and the cultural vehicles through which their sense of the orderly is expressed.

When this approach is applied to Islamic law – not just the use of oaths but the legal system as part of the entire cultural system – some intriguing implications suggest themselves. Thus, it can be argued that it is not any one element of the process of legal fact-finding, any more than it is simply the ritual act of reversing one's garments to turn a Moroccan drought into bounty, that makes the desired consequences flow. Rather, it is the coherence of the entire system – of prayers and rituals, beliefs and practices, judicial inquiry and subjective assessment, oral witnessing and divine oaths – that contributes to the acceptability of any one element within the cultural scheme. A ritual thus gains its meaning – its connectedness to and summation of its people's culture – not from one "rational" or "irrational" element alone, but from the way it structures the entire process into an expressive form, a total performance, that accords with a people's felt sense of things. And an oath, like a ritual, a play, or a dance, "works," because of its connections to the rest of its culture – because (in the Moroccan instance) it presumes that same emphasis on the personal found elsewhere in the court and the culture, because it expresses the desire to attach truth to a mere utterance in much the same way that anyone bargaining in the market-place of relations must validate his assertions, and because it creates consequences for relationships not by a physical act – of combat or ordeal – but by the mechanism that North Africans regard as the surest instrument for affecting the web of indebtedness that binds man to man and man to God – the statement, the word, the reliably witnessed utterance. Thus each element of the process of creating and discerning facts gains meaning not from its explanatory or practical effects alone, but from its embeddedness in a whole set of expressive symbols that cohere in a recognizable and acceptable way for the people whose lives are informed by them.

But there is another feature to legal systems like that of the qadi that lends them a quality which, though arguably present in ritual and art as well, is particularly heightened in the context of adjudication. For, as we have seen, a judge can by the very act of declaring something to be so actually makes it so. His role, in many instances, is thus like the third of those three kinds of baseball umpires that Hadley Cantril humorously spoke of in an early work on social psychology: the first is the umpire who says: "There's balls and there's strikes and I calls 'em as they are"; the second says: "There's balls and there's strikes and I calls 'em as I sees 'em"; but the third says: "There's balls and there's strikes and they ain't nothin' till *I* calls 'em." Like this last umpire the qadi can truly create reality. The word "reality" is used advisedly in this context because the word in Arabic for reality – *haqq* – is one of the central terms in the entire culture, embracing as it does the ideas of truth, obligation, right, and duty. *Haqq* thus summarizes the idea that it is the distribution of obligations that is the truest, the most real thing there is, and it is the qadi who is particularly capable of affecting this reality, these networks of obligation that men and women have forged by their own negotiations, with the single pronouncement that something is a fact. Like judges in some other cultures, he faces a society which is uncertain, chaotic, and indeterminate, and must create out of it an assessment that is itself quite determinate. Like our existential umpire, he is not likely to make his calls in a way or by criteria which, though they may remain rather fuzzy around the edges, lack any specificity whatsoever. Quite the contrary: his entire way of determining facts has, as we have seen, a distinct shape, indeed, a distinctly Moroccan and Islamic shape. For in addition to the emphasis, so central to the way relationships are formed in society at large, on personalism, oral evidence, and reliable witnessing for validation, there is a clear tendency in this system for the definition and determination of facts to be pushed down and away from the qadi to those highly localized personnel and procedures – the notaries and experts, the witnesses and customary practices – on which relationships themselves depend for their coherence.

Moreover, as will be argued in the next chapter, it is because the modes of reasoning employed in court and culture lay stress on the consequences of acts over their antecedents and because the central goal of the law is to place people on the track of negotiating their own relationships that the justice of the qadi is not predominantly dependent on formalities of procedure or courtroom style, judicially articulated levels of proof or internally refined bodies of legal doctrine. Rather, the Moroccan court captures the indeterminacy of Moroccan society in that society's own terms, embracing and containing variation by means of a culturally characteristic mode of reasoning and the religiously approved goal of encouraging men to contract their own ties within the limits set down by God. In turning, then, to the cultural as well as the legal aspects of the modes of reasoning, the assumptions about others' minds, and the implicit idea of justice found in contemporary Morocco it becomes possible to see the qadi as neither an arbitrary adjudicator nor an enigmatic oracle but as one whose words and actions afford a fascinating entry to his entire culture.

Plates

Plate 1

The *Maqamat*, or "Assemblies" of Abu Muhammed al-Qasim ibn Ali al-Hariri (1054–1122) contain numerous stories of wise or gullible qadis. The narrator, al-Harith, travels across the Middle East and is received by learned men while the trickster figure, Abu Zayd of Saruj, appears in many disguises and places, often at the side of a qadi and following the litigants out of court. The Assemblies were the subject of numerous illustrations, most dating from the thirteenth and fourteenth centuries. They have been collected and annotated in Oleg Grabar, *The Illustrations of the Maqamat* (Chicago: University of Chicago Press, 1984).

In one such assembly, the eighth, an old man and a youth appear before the qadi of Ma'arrah. The old man claims to have lent the youth a beautiful slave girl who was then mistreated, while the youth claims that the old man detained as compensation a male slave of excellent quality belonging to the youth. Sensing the enigmatic aspects of their story the qadi bids them speak plainly, and the old man admits he actually loaned the youth a needle that was then broken and retained in turn an eyebrow pencil belonging to the youth. In elaborate and plaintive verse the old man characterizes himself as being so poor he cannot even afford the loss of a needle, and the qadi, taking pity on both, offers them money and bids them depart in peace. Later, growing suspicious, he sends for both and promises no punishment if they will admit their deceit. The old man then acknowledges that the youth is actually his son and that they fabricated the dispute in order to wheedle money out of the judge:

> By every art, and with every aim:
> by earnest if it prosper, and if not, by jest.
> That we may draw forth a drop for our thirsty lot,
> and consume our life in wretched virtual.

The qadi praises the old man for the brilliance of his speech and releases both upon their promise to work no further deceit. Illustration: National Bibliothek, Vienna, A.F.9, folio 30ˇ.Text: Thomas Chenery (trans.), *The Assemblies of Al Hariri*, vol. I (London: Williams and Norgate, 1867), pp. 145–51.

Plate 2

"[In the ninth assembly of al-Hariri], Harith in his wanderings comes to Alexandria, and, in accordance with his custom, makes the acquaintance of the Qadi, who, as appears in the sequel, is a good-natured and benevolent man. One evening, in winter, the Qadi is distributing the public alms, when an ill-looking old man is brought in by a young and handsome woman who accuses him of having married her on false pretenses. She declares that he had deceived her father by giving out that he has an excellent trade as a pearl-merchant; that he has been incautiously accepted, and that now, when it was too late, she has discovered that he has no business at all. Moreover, he had taken all her dress and furniture, piece by piece, and sold it to keep himself in idleness, leaving her and her child to starve. The Qadi is indignant, and threatens to send the husband to prison, unless he can clear himself of the charge. The defendant is in no way disconcerted, but at once improvises some elegant verses, in which he admits his poverty, and that he had sold his wife's effects, but denies that he has deceived her in calling himself a "pearl-stringer," for the pearls which he meant were the pearls of thought, by stringing which into elegant poems he had been accustomed to make a large income from the liberality of the rich and noble. Now, however, times were changed: war and trouble had come upon the earth, and a race of niggards had succeeded the generous patrons of the old days. The Qadi accepts the excuse, bids the woman submit herself to her husband, and gives them some of the alms money; on receiving which the old man triumphantly carries off his wife. Harith had discovered that it was Abu Zayd, but was afraid to tell the Qadi, because in that case he might have to decline to relieve such an imposter. But when he is gone, Harith cannot forbear suggesting that he should be followed and some news of him brought back. A messenger is sent and returns quickly to say that he found Abu Zayd dancing and singing in joy at his success. The Qadi treats the affair as a good jest; and declares that if he had known who he was he would have been still more liberal." Illustration: Bibliothèque Nationale, Paris, ms. arabe 5847, folio 25. Text: Thomas Chenery (trans.), *The Assemblies of Al Hariri*, vol. I (London: Williams and Norgate, 1867), pp. 151–52.

فانتهبه القاضي احد امنائه وامر بالنجس على ابايه فاليت ان رجع مسعد واقهقر

مقهقها فقال للقاضي مهيم يا مريم فقال لقد عاينت عجبا وسمعت ما انشاء طرب بافعاله ماذا اراب

وما الذي دعيت فقال انا بذل الشيخ مدخج بصر يديه وكان لفز رطله ويعرد بل بشغيفه ونول

كن اصلي بلية من وفاج شرية

وازور   واذق التجن لولا حاكم الاسكندرية

Plate 3 (a) and (b)

A bedraggled old man appears in the thirty-seventh assembly of al-Hariri and complains to the qadi that his son is disobedient – "when I spoke plain, he shuffled in his speech, when I kindled a fire, he put it out, and when I roasted, he scattered ashes." The son denies the charge saying that he had always been taught by his father not to be covetous, but now his father inveighs upon him to beg for their living. The father responds that when needs demand one must depend on the generosity of the wealthy, and he recalls how the son himself had once said: "Sit not content with distress and suffering hunger's pangs, that people may say he is high-minded and patience full." The son replies that people nowadays are without concern for the poor, but the qadi, proud of the reputation of the men of his region for generosity, responds by himself bestowing a sum of money on the pair. The narrator, suspicious that the entire story may have been concocted to elicit money from the judge, follows the pair out of court but is unable to establish with certainty their identity or motives.

Illustrations: (a) British Library, London, or. 1200, folio 120ˇ; (b) Bibliothèque Nationale, Paris, ms. arabe 5847, folio 114ˇ. Text: F. Steingass (trans.), *The Assemblies of Al Hariri*, vol. II (London: Royal Asiatic Society, 1898), pp. 83–89.

غير مقاد ... فلم يكن لك ... شرارة أو وحيا ... حتى احضر
علام ... خانه ضرغام ... فقال الشيخ أيد الله القاضى وعكمه

ما التغاضى ... أن أظهرا الكلة أذى ... الشرف الصلى

Plate 4

A husband and wife appear in the fortieth assembly of al-Hariri before a notoriously stingy judge. The couple carry on a furious series of allegations about each other's misconduct until the qadi, feeling himself visited with "an incurable disease and crushing calamity," if he turns either party aside, bemoans his ever having become a judge. He commands the usher to "rid me of these two babblers and silence their tongues with two gold coins; then dismiss the company, and close the gate proclaiming that this is an ill-omened day and that the Qadi is in mourning on it, so that no litigant may come into my presence." The usher gives the couple their coins, but suspecting a ruse praises their craftiness and warns that not every qadi will at all times listen to such rhetoric. "So they said to him: 'There is not thy like of Ushers, and thanks are due to thee,' wherewith they got up and stalked away with their two gold pieces, roasting the heart of the Qadi on two fires." Illustration: Bibliothèque Nationale, Paris, ms. arabe 5847, folio 126; text: F. Steingass (trans.), *The Assemblies of Al Hariri*, vol. II (London: Royal Asiatic Society, 1898), pp. 101–108.

Plate 5 (a) and (b)

Public scribes are often employed by litigants, as well as ordinary letter-writers, to prepare papers for court proceedings. Some who possess religious or magical knowledge prepare amulets and inscribed phrases used in supplications for divine assistance or affairs of the heart. These scribes, like the clerks who serve in the courts, have deep historic roots in the institutions of Islamic law and society. The clerk and litigant in (a) come from an illustration of the twenty-sixth assembly of al-Hariri (Bibliothèque Nationale, Paris, ms. arabe 5847, folio 79).

Photograph (b) shows a scribe at work in the public market-place of a Moroccan city around 1930 (*Morocco: A Country of Islam*. Casablanca: Editions Maurice Bory, n.d.).

Plate 6

In the late nineteenth century, European artists portrayed scenes from Middle Eastern life – usually of the harem or the hunt – in highly romanticized terms. It was in this style that the Spanish artist Tomás Moragas (1837–1906) approached the theme of Arab justice in his 1878 painting *An Arab Tribunal*, an engraving of which appeared in the *Illustrated London News* of May 24, 1884. The unlikely scene and the following description appended to the engraving show clearly the orientalist style and colonialist sentiment of the day:

"[W]e should take it that the scene is laid in Morocco. A court of judicial investigation is being held by the Cadi with six competent assessors, one of them an old white-bearded Sheikh, for the trial of a half-naked Arab charged with murder. The judges do not sit upon a Bench, but squat on a sumptuous carpet, while the prisoner lies on the rough stone pavement, with his hands fastened in two holes in a heavy wooden machine, constructed on the same plan as that of a pair of stocks for the feet. The principal witness for the prosecution seems to be giving evidence and pointing to a blood-stained "abayah," the cotton garment worn by the deceased when he was killed, which is pierced with terrible gashes by the murder's knife. Several officers of the military guard, on horseback, are in attendance to preserve order in the court, and one is beating back, with his stick, the crowd of spectators thronging too near the judges. The architectural ornamentation of the palace gate and windows is accurately drawn, and the picture may be pronounced an excellent work of art."

3

Reason, intent, and the logic of consequence

It was in November of 1608 that King James I of England, a monarch who prided himself on his great learning and wisdom, confronted the greatest jurist and parliamentarian of the day, Sir Edward Coke, about Coke's belief in the privileged status of judges as the sole interpreters of the common law. Since God had bestowed Reason on all civilized people and since English law claims to be founded on Reason, why, James inquired, could not any intelligent and exceptional man – a king, for example – be qualified to interpret the law? Coke responded to this threat to judicial supremacy with the following argument:

> True it is that God has endowed Your Majesty with excellent science, and great endowments of nature; but Your Majesty is not learned in the law of this your realm of England, and causes which concern the life, or inheritance, or goods, or fortune of your subjects, are not to be decided by natural reason, but by the artificial reason and judgement of the law, which law is an art which requires long study and experience before that a man can attain to the cognizance of it.

Coke's argument that law proceeds by means of what he called "artificial reason" seems so apt a characterization of western forms of legal reasoning that we may have a tendency to think it universally true. We are used to seeing words of ordinary meaning – words like "negligent," "willful," or "intentional" – become terms of art when employed by lawyers and judges, and we may accordingly characterize many instances of judicial logic as strained or intended to mask a hidden purpose. Indeed, one has only to try drawing up one's own will and then present this seemingly straightforward document to a lawyer to see the wonders of legal language – like some reverse alchemy – transform "children" into "the issue of my body" or watch our highest courts comparing generations of cases in order to decide if the legislature meant to include a capon as a chicken or a biplane as a vehicle in order to experience the peculiar use of language and logic in our law. That a given legal system should, as we have seen, develop its own assumptions or fictions to deal with that which can never really be determined precisely or that, as we shall see later, the development of such artificial reason should be deeply entwined with the political context of the law's reach is of obvious importance to an understanding of legal styles of thought and use of language. What is perhaps less obvious, however, is that a legal system may, by its goals, its sources of legitimacy, and its particular relationship with the larger culture of which it is a part, evince very little indeed in the way of artificial reasoning, so much of its authority and impact being dependent on its incorporation, within a distinctive institutional context, of the very same modes of thought and substantive results that characterize a host of domains of everyday life. Indeed, it is precisely the argument here that not only do the modes of Moroccan judicial fact-finding discussed earlier fit with – indeed share with – the broader culture their characteristic emphases on reliable witnessing, validation of non-truth-bearing utterances, and oath allocation based on rational cultural assessments, but the same is essentially true when we turn to the nature of judicial reasoning, where the mode and goal of the court's thinking is extraordinarily similar to that which is found in most other domains of Moroccan daily life.

This problem of the nature of judicial reasoning and its connections to the world of politics and culture is, of course, common to many developed systems of law. At least three main approaches are discernible when forms of legal reasoning are viewed across cultures and times. One is for a set of rules to be articulated and for judges to couch their decisions, however they may actually be reached, in such a way as to give the appearance that they have been derived by a simple process of deduction from the announced rules. A second is for the judge to gauge an individual's actions against a broad standard, like "reasonableness" or "due care," which can incorporate everyday experience and for which the judge must now, by recourse to prior decisions or applicable legislation, measure the particular facts presented him and pronounce upon their correct categorization.

A third approach, which may employ elements of the first two, consists of the rules being drawn in such a way as to justify a wide range of individual results from which the judge may choose. If particular procedures are followed or if limiting precepts are not overstepped considerable leeway for results may be permitted without the results themselves or the substantive rules from which they are generated always having to appear precisely similar. In the latter instance rules serve more as guidelines and reasoning consists in the establishment of an individual result within the ambit of the acceptable. Indeed, while it may in some instances be true of other orientations as well, it is a particular characteristic of this third mode of reasoning that people will accord legitimacy to their courts not because judgments are given the appearance of being uniquely correct but because they simply stay close enough to what their citizens are prepared to accept. Just as the economically rational man may be able to live with either of two contradictory rules or results if the terms of analysis fall within the range of leeway allowed by his mode of thought, so, too, a judge whose system of law has not jeopardized its legitimacy by eliminating culturally acceptable alternatives does not always have to be right – he must only avoid being too clearly wrong.

Now, when we look at the justice of the qadi in the light of this highly schematized array of alternatives, an argument suggests itself that will serve as the focal point for the present discussion. It is, quite simply, that the qadi, rather like the third model, operates within a range of acceptable results and that these results are minimally shaped in their outer perimeter by the small number of specific rules laid down in the Quran and are, to a far greater degree, subsequently dependent on an assessment of the consequences that various actions have for the construction of interpersonal obligations within the community. Of no less critical importance is the idea that the central goal of the law is to set people back on a track of negotiating their own relationships, an orientation that supports a mode of judicial reasoning by which constant reference is made to the local practices of the people and to the application of those same modes of reasoning by which these negotiated relationships are themselves rendered possible. It means, in short, that the reasoning of the qadi, far from having to develop artificially to assert its legitimacy or political independence, is constantly embroiled in the assessment of situated actions through many of the same modes of thought that one finds throughout all domains of Moroccan life. To see what the implications of this claim are for an understanding of Islamic legal organization, we must turn to an analysis of the particular ways in which the qadi employs his reason in the determination of a judicial result.

Students of Islamic law invariably begin their description by noting that there are four classic sources of Islamic law, namely, the Quran, the authoritative Traditions about what the Prophet himself said or did, the process of reasoning analogically from instances cited in these basic texts to those confronting the judge for the first time, and the general agreement or consensus of the community – or at least its leading members – about how a given problem should be handled. But it is interesting to note that each of these sources is quite different from the others. The Quran is the only source of law that is written, and it earns its special status by being the exact spoken word of God as reduced to writing by the Prophet, who was himself illiterate. Unlike, for example, the Old Testament, the Quran contains relatively few rule-like statements of law, and those it does recount are designated as "the claims of God," all else, the entitlements and obligations of man, being left largely to humanity's own determination so long as people do not overstep the limits set down by God. The Traditions, by contrast, were recorded after the Prophet's death, and like the evocation of valid evidence they center on oral transmission through a chain of named relators back to one who may be regarded as a reliable witness of what the Prophet actually said or did. Thus while these Traditions constitute substantive guidance, they mainly depend for their authority on a mode of reasoning – on oral witnessing by those who are personally discernible as reliable. Analogic reasoning, or *qiyas*, is entirely a mode of thought, while consensus, *ijma*ʿ, works from the Tradition in which the Prophet says that "my community will not agree in error" and allows general practice, at least as articulated by community leaders, to establish the legal standards. Note, too, that in theory custom is not a source of law in Islam but that by each of the three means other than the Quran it can and does receive legal implementation. What is particularly striking, however, is that at the very outset Islam takes as sources of the law things that are really methods or techniques – modes of reasoning or of "discovering" law – and that, with the exception of Quranic injunctions, there is a great deal of malleability and personalism built into these sources.

Contemporary qadis in Morocco, as elsewhere in the Middle East, are very much the heirs to the sort of method implied in these classical sources of Islamic law even though a number of particulars have changed over the course of the centuries. When announcing an opinion or recording it in the court records, qadis rarely refer to the Quran or Traditions. Since the adoption of the Code of Personal Status shortly after Independence in 1956, Moroccan qadis are far more likely to cite the relevant provision in the code and simply to state the relation of the facts, as developed by the notaries and experts, to this new code. But however much the facts may be shaped for the qadi by lower-ranking personnel in the court and however much the code may detail particular approaches to a number of standard issues, the process of judicial reasoning cannot be reduced to the mechanical application of code to circumstance. For as we have already seen in the development of evidence, the establishment of facts is itself a process dependent on the creative application of common cultural assumptions to specific, legally cognizable events. So, too, in the application of reason.

Take, for example, the not uncommon situation in which there is no clear provision in the code or for which the range of judicial leeway is specifically licensed by legislation. In such a case the modern qadi may indeed resort to a form of analogic reasoning. In one such instance, a qadi had been presented with a notarized document in which twelve witnesses testified in an inheritance dispute that they knew the plaintiff to have been lawfully married to the deceased. The defense claimed that a number of the witnesses were not from the village where the wedding was said to have occurred or were not present when the wedding happened many years earlier. Given this assertion by the defense several of the plaintiff's witnesses did an about-face and claimed that they had never actually testified to knowledge of the wedding itself, only to having been around at the time it was said to have occurred. If their testimony were removed, the plaintiff's case would have suffered greatly since it would have dropped the number of witnesses necessary for this form of proof below the requisite twelve. The plaintiff, however, responded by arguing that a denial as to some of one's testimony was not analogous to a complete retraction and that if what the witnesses claimed to have heard from others about the occurrence of the wedding nevertheless had probative value, the qadi should continue to regard them as valid witnesses for purposes of the notarized document. Scholarly opinions supporting their respective positions were presented to the qadi by both sides, but the qadi favoured the plaintiff's position, stating that although others might see it differently, this case was more like a situation in which some of the facts are stated with certainty than one in which previous assertions have been categorically denied. Since the witnesses testified as to features that were common for weddings at that time and in that part of the countryside and since a retraction embraces the idea of denying even the knowledge of things that would appear quite credible, it would, the qadi concluded, be quite inappropriate to analogize the shift from personal to hearsay knowledge as equivalent to a full retraction.

An opinion such as this clearly shows how a series of factors cohere in a single act of judicial reasoning. For not only is there a clear choice of one analogy over another, but a distinctive set of techniques and assumptions themselves shape the process and the goal of the choice made. Here, for instance, we see the court having recourse to a presumption that is distinctive to Islamic law, namely, the idea that an assertion of a "positive" fact should take precedence over a "negative" one – that is, all other things being equal, that testimony about something having occurred should be favored over testimony that it did not. In this particular case the qadi took as a positive assertion the circumstantial details about which the witnesses still admitted hearing, even though they withdrew their claim to any more direct knowledge, and used this presumption to thwart any implication that the witnesses were now saying that no wedding ever occurred.

Tracing the logic of what qadis designate as positive or negative leads one through a series of instances which do not immediately seem to cohere in any rational way. Testimony that a sale occurred is seen as positive and a claim that nothing has occurred to alter prior circumstances is designated negative; but (with the exception of a mother asserting custody over her child) testimony impeaching another's character is regarded as positive and hence to be favoured while testimony tending to support one's character is demarcated negative. From an analysis of numerous cases and from discussions with court officials a systematic quality and a rationale to these presumptions may be suggested. For if it is true that the predominant goal of the qadi is not to regulate the details of all relationships but, particularly where the Quran or the code are not unyieldingly explicit, to set people back on the track of negotiating their own relationships with one another, then it appears that all those events designated as positive, and thus judicially favored, are those in which a shift has occurred in the balance of obligations between the parties. By recognizing that such alterations are indeed the normal course of things and by favoring this position over claims that no alteration has occurred, the court gives legal support to the new set of obligations and imposes no further shifts beyond those the parties may subsequently choose to arrange for themselves.

Thus marriages are reaffirmed, sales taken as probable occurrences, and – interestingly – the likelihood acknowledged that if a man has not been able to establish his reputation for credibility before an actual case arises he will likely be of poor moral character and hence an unreliable witness.

Here, too, we can see an excellent example of how cultural assumption, legal approach, and substantive law are all deeply entwined. For the determination of positive versus negative assertions is indissolubly linked to local concepts and local customs, even though, at least in classical Islamic thought, custom was not a source of law. We have already seen a number of instances where legal presumptions are really little more than the judicial recognition of local assumptions. Thus one could point to the presumption that the father of a child conceived in a marriage is indeed the husband of the mother, the presumption in favor of a guardian's qualifications, or the presumption that a mortally wounded man is truthful when designating his attacker. Legal prescriptions may afford direct insight into the ways in which we assess the character and qualities of various kinds of people in our society. In the United States, for example, ordinary witnesses are permitted to testify to the conclusion that another was "drunk," but they are not allowed to testify that another was "in love" – the latter being somehow too private to be discerned, at least without psychiatric expertise. In Morocco, there are records of cases in which qadi's courts have explicitly presumed that since it is the normal course of things for Jews to engage in the practice of usury, that may be presumed in any particular case until proven otherwise. There is even one perfectly charming case in which a qadi in 1916 held that since government administrators are normally dishonest, a defendant administrator should be required to swear a holy oath in support of his assertions in order to rebut this perfectly reasonable presumption. It should perhaps be noted, however, that the appellate court, which possessed either a different view of human nature or a less developed sense of humor, overruled the qadi on this point. In general one need not be able to sort out with certainty whether these kinds of presumptions arose in the law as convenient ways of accounting for uncertainties and then spread into the culture or, as is probably the case here, that they spread from the culture into law in order for us to see the close correspondence that exists between Islamic law and culture on these points. More intriguing yet for its cultural and legal similarity is the form of logic employed when a series of these features are linked to one another.

It was noted earlier that from the very outset of a case the qadi always expresses interest in the social origins of those appearing before him – where they come from, with whom they are attached, what customs their background suggests they would most likely employ in arranging their ties to others. It is information vital to that predominant reality of Moroccan life, the distribution of obligations among individuals. And just as in ordinary social life, where one feature of social origins suggests by implication a series of attendant features, so, too, the qadi draws logical conclusions in a culturally characteristic way from matters of personal background. Thus to know that someone is an urban Arab whose family has its origins in the town and practices a given occupation suggests that one possesses substantive knowledge about certain other men and their dealings, that one has a wide range of connections that may bear on one's ties to the contending party in the present case, and that these interlocking ties may have a particular impact on the way the qadi's decision will affect others and be supported by them. It is this set of assumptions – this code of cultural entailments – that is drawn upon by the qadi in making his connections. These assumptions and their modes of institutionalization have, of course, varied over the course of time. There exists, for example, a long tradition in Islamic scholarship and judicial practice of assessing another's character and actions by means of an elaborate science of physiognomy: until recent times the qadi could call on an expert in the field who would determine a person's claimed background or mode of forming relationships on the basis of physical traits suggestive of social background. Even now this mode of analysis may enter paternity suits and contribute to the rejection of modern medical testimony. Indeed, it is interesting to note that the same word in Arabic – *asel* – means not only "social origins" and "sources of law," but that form of logical reasoning which takes note of the consequences that normally flow from any given trait or act.

This legal application of a cultural assumption is also related to the common belief – again, given judicial articulation – that the harm a person does is a function of his or her social position, and therefore to know the latter is to calculate the former, and, more to the point, what to do about it. Thus, it is believed that an educated man does more harm by an illegal act than one who is uneducated because the former is a guide for others – one upon whom others should depend, one whose actions embrace extensive networks and implications. Similarly, men believe that women are by their nature more prone to be guided by passion than by reason and must, therefore, be restrained from those acts that man may perform more readily for fear of the chaos that follows when sexual attraction is given the opportunity to follow its ineluctable course. As will be seen when consideration is given to the Moroccan concepts of justice, qadis invariably say that no two cases are precisely the same because the people are not exactly the same, but that it is only common sense to realize that a man who "has *asel*," who is of some social position, can do more harm than a "nobody" and that the implications one draws from knowledge of background are central to choosing appropriate remedies.

Inquiries about social identity are thus firmly linked to a point that will shortly begin to emerge even more sharply in our discussion, namely, that this is a legal system whose constant emphasis is not on a series of antecedent concepts but on evaluating the consequences of people's actions. In the way that evidence is adduced, in the way presumptions are formulated, and in the way entailments are implied the constant focus of Moroccans – in the law and in the culture – is on the consequences of actions in the realm of human relationships. This feature is particularly evident when we look at the way the qadis of Morocco, in the course of articulating their judicial method, have developed a unique body of legal literature and applied it through a distinctive concept of the public good.

Throughout the course of Islamic history it has been common to find the presentation to the qadi of scholarly opinions on particular points of law as well as inquiries about matters of law being sent to such scholars in the absence of an actual legal proceeding. Elsewhere in the Middle East famous instances of such advisory opinions, or *fatwas*, have included those sought to determine if it was permissible to use the new technique of printing to produce copies of the Quran or whether particular forms of nationalistic activity violated any Islamic precept. There have also been some wonderfully humorous inquiries, as, for example, the time the great medieval jurisconsult Ibn Taimiyya was approached by an illiterate Bedouin who inquired: "Is it permissible (O great and learned sir!) to ride upon a camel – that has drunk wine?"

In Morocco, even at the present time, it is not at all uncommon for litigants to request opinions from those who are noted for their religious learning. To the facts presented them by one party the scholar will apply the approaches developed by generations of students of Malikite Islamic law and exercise his own interpretive powers within the framework of traditional legal reasoning to suggest a specific decision to the qadi. Certainly in the past the result may have been similar to that of certain parts of the Arab east, where a reciprocal relation existed between the qadi's judgments and the scholar's advisory opinions. As one analyst has put it: "Fatwas utilize concrete descriptions as *given* instances necessitating interpretation in theory; judgments address cases as *problematic* instances that are themselves in need of interpretation." In Morocco, *fatwas* no doubt helped to keep the process of interpretation open and gave fuller support to the same modes of reasoning being applied by the court. But there was also greater scope for Moroccan qadis to perform some of the textual interpretation that elsewhere may have been undertaken by scholars, for they had at their command three implements of great significance: a body of actual judicial decisions, a concept of the public utility, and an emphasis – characteristic of Malikite law generally – on the intentions that inform the acts of a given individual.

Although one finds throughout the Muslim world collections of scholarly opinions – often formulaically prescribed, even in poetic rhyme – what one does not find are collections of reported cases or statements about what qadis have done about concrete issues in particular jurisdictions. The exception, however, is North Africa. For here we do find not only a concept of attending to actual judicial practice, but collections that include, in addition to responses and formularies, instances of particular judicial decisions. This body of literature, known as the 'amal writings, only came to western attention in the early part of this century, and its role in Moroccan law has been the source of some dispute. On the one hand reference to what other qadis have decided runs counter to the basic design of classical Islamic jurisprudence. By that theory judges have no right to pronounce on what the law should be; they should, at most, only extend the law from such definite sources as the Quran and traditions by means of analogies, and even here should be guided by scholarly opinion. The relation of scholarship to practice in this image is that in which, as one commentator has put it, the chair is not only more comfortable but more influential than the bench. On the other hand, we find the jurists of North Africa, particularly Morocco, distinguishing away scholarly opinion in certain instances and placing judicial decisions at the pinnacle of the legal process. What is particularly intriguing is that here, too, the process makes a good deal of sense when seen in the light of the culturally characteristic way it works.

Faced with a case that did not squarely fall within the ambit of the universally recognized, a Moroccan qadi, looking about for guidance, would take note of several different kinds of opinions. He could, for example, choose to follow what is called the "dominant opinion" (*mashhur*), the approach which most commentators and collections have adopted and which is, therefore, the best approach available. A minority approach, called an "isolated" or "preferred" approach (*rajih*) may, however, be relied upon instead. This will be the opinion of a particularly well-respected authority – scholar or judge – who has decided, in an actual case, that it is better for the common good that the dominant approach be set aside in favor of a decision that is more able to achieve a socially useful goal or avoid a harm that the implementation of the dominant approach may unintentionally engender. If a qadi applies such a distinctive approach, or if he favors another's isolated approach over the dominant one, he clearly must do it by bringing to bear precisely the same aspects of personal forcefulness that we have seen at work in other domains of Moroccan culture. He must show, as we will see in a moment, that his assessment of the consequences of this approach will be beneficial, he will have to possess the reputation and connections to make this personal approach stick, and he will have to present it in a way that demonstrates conformity to the Quran and basic sources of the law. In some instances, of course, the qadi's use of another's isolated approach is made more acceptable by showing that at least three judges have used this approach in much the same way he intends to, and we can see in such instances how a distinctive approach may come to be the prevailing one. But in many instances it is clear that what the judge is doing is applying, in highly localized circumstances, a concept of social utility that may differ not only from the approach of some other jurisdictions but the dominant practice acknowledged in almost all other regions.

What, then, does this notion of social utility really mean? In Islamic law, particularly as practiced in Morocco, one frequently encounters the concepts of *istihsan* and *istislah*. Both are forms of legal reasoning by means of analogy, but each incorporates the idea that analogies may be drawn with a clear eye to the social well-being at large rather than to a strict set of logically required results. On its face, it would appear to be a device whereby a judge might get around all but the most clear-cut of Quranic propositions to implement an approach he regards as desirable. But neither the concept of public utility nor its actual invocation appears to be without surrounding principles that limit its application. To see how the qadi reasons his way through matters using the concept of public good in combination with judicial practice and local custom, it may be helpful to describe an actual case. It is, I fear, yet another of those disputes that Hugo Grotius, bored by the cases presented him as a young lawyer in the early 1700s, wearily described as being "about dripping eaves or party walls," but since the real point here is about judicial reasoning, I will try to make the details as painless as possible.

In 1946 a group of people came before the qadi in Fez. They said that their predecessors had owned, in common with another man, a building that was divided into two parts. A passageway existed between the two sections that allowed, in effect, a back door to the shop that their precursor had established in his half of the structure. Given the incredible rabbit warren of streets in Fez one can readily understand the convenience such an additional access route might afford. Forty years ago, however, the passageway was blocked up. There was no indication that any complaint was ever made about this state of affairs, and several successive heirs used the shop and lived over it without contesting the closure. Not, that is, until the present heirs came into possession of the store. They immediately sought to have the passageway reopened. Experts sent by the qadi noted that there clearly had been a door there once – the lintel and pillars were still perfectly visible – and the qadi, in a characteristically conclusive and uninformative written opinion, held that the heirs did indeed have the right to reopen it. It is the appellate court – itself, of course, an institution that had not existed before colonial times, but wholly comprised of Muslim judges – which invoked a notion of the social good. In sustaining the qadi's judgment the court cited a fourteenth-century scholar who said that "the public good is to be found in continuity, the preservation of what already exists." The problem, of course, was in fixing which state of affairs to continue – the forty-year-old blockage or the maintenance of a passageway whose closure had never been explicitly ratified by the plaintiff's benefactor. The court, however, used the evidence of the earlier doorway to argue that the original owners must have meant there to be such a point of access. They even cited an unnamed poet who admonished "after our death/respect the traces that we left," and following references to other collections of opinions the court ruled that since openness is to be favored over closure the traces of the earlier opening preserved to the heirs the right to reopen the passageway.

Now this opinion, which has everything in it from ancient commentary to orphaned poetry, rests, in part, on the idea that it is best for society to preserve the existing state of things and that absent a clear change in the obligations of the parties involved the earlier state of things should be preferred over the more recent. Undoubtedly the court could have decided the other way round – it even cited the most famous pupil of the founder of the Malikite school of Islamic law, who said that the point was undecided since the master himself had never spoken to this issue. But the court did review other legal sources and found none of them conclusive, did link itself to the statements of other commentators, and did adduce as socially useful a principle of the continuity of established relationships over one that rewrites the original agreement. What they did not do was cite other cases or couch matters simply in terms of rights and duties. And the elaborateness of their opinion suggests their desire to show that their approach, though deviating from some collected opinions, was sustainable by others. The result is a pattern that is frequently replicated in Moroccan legal reasoning: the judicial choice among reported approaches taken by well-known authorities is itself informed, through a principle of the socially useful, by local practice even where that practice may run contrary to the dominant opinion about how such a situation should be resolved.

But the case is also revealing for the interplay of private and social considerations. It has often been said that Islamic law is a law about and for individuals: like Islam itself the religious law asks whether an individual's actions are or are not permissible rather than attempting to decide whether the community at large possesses interests that differ from the moral and legal evaluation of individual acts. The case of the blocked entry would seem to support this interpretation. The court speaks of the intention of the benefactor and the need to honor the situation he left behind, while in other cases it clearly supports the maintenance of private agreements. But the court here also speaks of favoring openness over closure, and in many other instances clearly applies presumptions that favor the maintenance of the status quo as a way of avoiding social chaos. It is not, then, that broader social interests are unknown or that specific concepts of social utility are absent from Islamic law as practiced in Morocco. Rather it is true that even the social interest is conceptualized in terms of maintaining peaceful private interaction: what is good for the individual is good for society. What is missing, until at least the beginning of western influence, is the institutionalization of the public as an entity whose interests might be assessed like those of a person. In the absence of the idea that corporate entities might constitute jural personalities the social interest enters the law as a localized interpretation of the legal status of particular named persons and their highly personalized acts. The choice of a preferred judicial approach over that which is more commonly employed thus draws upon the idea that the social good is served when local practice serves as the limit for comprehending the relations individuals have chosen to form with each other.

The qadi thus raises the assessment of local consequences to the legally supportable through reasons and concepts that grant his act legitimacy. Examples of this process abound. One could point to interpretations from previous centuries arguing that even though the clause in a marriage contract allowing a woman to initiate a divorce is granted by the husband voluntarily, the fact that local custom regards such a clause as having been given in exchange for a lower bride-price means that the contract should receive the stricter enforcement of an agreement that was actually bargained for. Or one could point to more recent instances where the qadi refused a rural woman's claim against her former husband for the cost of hospital delivery of their child because birth at home is customary for such women, even though most commentors include all birth expenses among those to which a woman is entitled. In each instance, the process of weighing alternatives through the grid of attested opinion, social utility, and local practice shapes and even limits the decisions of the qadi. His focus is not on substantive doctrines or the factual similarities and differences with prior cases, but on an assessment of consequences – on the repercussions for the networks of ties that people possess, or should be free to contract, in face-to-face dealings. Just as the thrust of judicial organization and the determination of facts constantly involves the tendency to propel matters down to the locally defined and locally derived, so, too, the mode of judicial reasoning channels the judge's thinking not to the level of ever more refined modes of analysis – ever more "artificial reasoning" – or to the elaboration of court-created doctrine, but to filling up broad propositions with local meaning or even allowing the local to govern the specifics set forth by noted sources.

It is a system which, borrowing from a seminal distinction made by John Dewey, can be said to work by a logic of consequence rather than a logic of antecedents. Dewey used this distinction to suggest that many systems of logic relate particular circumstances back to a set of antecedent concepts or assumptions and find some way to make the former fit with the latter. He thought, however, that western legal systems would be better advised, if principled continuity was to be preserved, to look at the consequences of matters and allow these assessments to take precedence over the attempt to make everything fit with some claimed antecedent. His prescription was, in a sense, an actual description of the state of things in Islamic culture – an approach that could work because the same focus on consequences informs social and legal thought in much the same way. Thus, we have seen that Moroccans stress a person's impact on networks of obligation, regard as truth-bearing only that which has affected actual relationships by being validated, and conceive of time itself not as evidence of prior principles evincing their ineluctable forces at work in the world of humankind but as packets of relationship, the revelation of what is true about men through the enumerated contexts of their situated ties. The result is an emphasis on the observable impact of actions, on the orderly negotiation of human relationships, and on the perpetuation not of antecedent concepts but consequent interdependency. That is why, too, we can find an early jurist emphasizing local consequences over the retention of doctrinal consistency when he says "Once the argument of the opinion adopted in judicial practice becomes clear to you (O Judge!) it becomes your duty to issue judgment in accordance with it, for adjudicating contrary to the judicial practice leads to civil strife and great corruption."

Nowhere does the emphasis on social consequence in the law and culture of Morocco reveal itself with more intriguing force than in the question of how assessments are made of another's state of mind, the question of intentionality. In the west it is generally taken as a common-sense fact that while no one can have direct access to the mind of another, one's inner state is, if not the fundamental site of one's truest being, at least an indispensable element without whose consideration a full understanding of human actions is necessarily incomplete. We may speak of that inner self as a hidden grotto, yet seek through arts both literary and enchanted its ultimate recesses and secrets; we may characterize it as a realm known only by the devil, yet bend the efforts of our science and machines to ferret out its telltale pulse and suppressed design. For us, unlike Gertrude Stein's characterization of Oakland, there really is a *there* there. For the people of Morocco – indeed, perhaps of the Arab world generally – the idea of something that can be called human intent is also manifestly real. But just as our idea of mind and intent are deeply entwined with changes in our vision of the person – from communal to romantic, from innate to emergent – so, too, the Arabs' vision of intent, and its social and legal implications, partakes of a style and interconnections distinctive to their own culture and times.

In Arabic, the word for intent is *niya*, a word that means not only "will," "volition," "plan," and "design" but "simple," "sincere," and "naïve." Where in the modern west intent is seen to lie within and to be sufficiently distinguishable from overt acts that we might ask both God and man to judge us by our intentions and not our deeds, in the Middle East, intent and act are thought to be so closely linked that one can read rather directly from a person's words and deeds the intent that lies within. To start each of the five daily prayers by stating one's intention is to manifest in the world the design of naïve submission to Allah; to discover another's many acts – the varied situations in which he or she has formed and enacted ties to others – is to discern that person's inner state. The result is a cultural assumption expressed in a characteristic style: that the individual possesses an inner driving force that directs actions but that until and unless it affects relationships in the world it is not merely indiscernible, it is truly unimportant. God, says the Prophetic Tradition, loves those who hide their sins – not because sinning is good but because social repercussions that risk civil strife are greatly to be feared and anything that does not, in this sense, come into the world is strictly between God and the individual. Once action follows it is indeed possible to know another's mind. Intent, far from being irrelevant when it enters the world of relationships, becomes one of the central features by which one talks about another. And that is so because words and deeds are connected directly to intent; to know the one is thus to know the other. This orientation is particularly visible in the realm of the qadi and his court.

In Islamic law the idea of intent figures importantly in a number of situations. The most intriguing, as in the west, is perhaps in the case of murder. In precolonial Morocco, as in other Muslim countries of that era, criminal acts were almost entirely matters of private dispute between the families of those involved or were issues taken before the political authorities rather than the qadi. But Islamic law as well as custom spoke to the issue of homicide and did so in a characteristic way. Killings that were designated as intentional could lead to lawful retaliation or punishment, as opposed to accidental killings which might require compensation. But how was intent determined? One of the main ways was by the weapon used: if a killing involved a weapon that was normally used for or likely to produce death – a knife, a spear, a gun – then the attacker was assumed to have meant to kill his or her victim. Use of an instrument normally regarded as nonlethal – a stick, for example – would lead to the reverse finding. It was not that intent was disregarded, but rather that it followed from the definition of the event.

Similarly, much turned on social background, past actions, and other social qualities of the accused. Using the code of cultural entailment referred to earlier, a judge could assess another's state of mind from the kind of background and events he had engaged in – an assessment, in essence, of character. In American criminal jurisprudence such an approach is generally regarded as grossly unfair: past convictions, for example, are not allowed as evidence in American courts unless they are directly connected to the specific offence in question or show a habit of repeating the same proscribed act. Moreover, in the United States only the defendant may initiate an assessment or his or her character unless it is for the limited purpose of impeaching credibility. Such restrictions make no sense to judges in Morocco, Whenever asked, they always say the same thing. In the words of one qadi: "If I question people, if I find out who they are and what they have done; I can always tell if they are lying; I can always tell their *niya*, their intent." A Saudi Arabian scholar has written: "The judge has to have an acute sense of observation; for example, just by looking at a suspect he should be able to tell what the man had concealed in his testimony." And the reason why judges believe this can be done is because they really do believe that to know one's background, appearance, and prior acts can indeed give one direct access to another's state of mind and hence the basis of additional acts in the world.

Thus, the Islamic judge does not set intent aside: he accepts it as being visible to the knowledgeable eye as we assume it may be visible when a person feeling embarrassed shows it on his or her skin through a blush. Such judges are not practicing a form of strict liability; they are not saying intent is irrelevant and punishment follows from proof of the act alone. That is the situation in American law when, for example, the fact is ignored that a man accused of the statutory rape of an under-age female swears she looked twenty-one years old and that she showed everyone a driver's license to prove it. Statutory rape is regarded as so harmful that no excuses will be allowed for its commission. Such a system may assert society's fears and values or, when applied to something like no-fault insurance, constitute a way of sharing the costs of common injuries. But Islamic law always regards the act as connected to the intent and thus preserves the idea that words and deeds actually reveal the hidden inner state of another. And since motives and intentions can themselves be shaped by the way others attribute them to us, such an emphasis may contribute greatly to the personalization of the social.

Intent therefore figures directly in a number of contemporary proceedings that take place before the qadi. Cases could be cited that say that when a man forms a trust fund his intent must govern its terms even when the words actually used in its creation seem to admit of an unambiguous interpretation. But when we look at how that intent is itself discerned, we come back again to the social background and other acts of the individual in question. Similarly, if one man pays another's lawful obligations without the other having requested it, the qadi may cite the idea that it is the normal order of things for people to part with their money intentionally and that so long as the payment was made with the intent of friendship and not to prejudice the other in some way, the debt must be repaid. And how is that intent made known? Again, through the personal circumstances of the individual.

A pattern thus emerges: a person's state of mind is available to others through his or her situated acts – occurrences that draw together the qualities of nature, background, and biography to make an inner state "obvious." The emphasis on intent thus personalizes the perception of the other in a way that might, from a western perspective, be taken as stereotypical, depersonalizing, and unfair, but which, in the Moroccan perception of the other, constitutes the truest assessment possible – the enactment of one's background and associations in the realm of the public. It is an emphasis common to the way Moroccans perceive one another as they try to predict behavior in social relations and try to negotiate the most favorable ties for themselves, and it is therefore an approach which, given legal application, seems to them enormously familiar, fair, and true.

It is thus easy to find much that is familiar to western eyes in Moroccan society and law yet fail to grasp the critical differences. We can see an emphasis on the individual and mistakenly equate it with the western notion of individual*ism*, of a self-directed and self-fashioning person whose inner, psychic structure generates a self that is, whatever its overt manifestations, deeply and truly private. And we could find in the Moroccan legal system a set of assumptions, different in kind, perhaps, but not all that different in level of abstraction, that guides judges who, like our own, compare and distinguish the case before them with those related in the available legal literature. Both approaches would, however, fall far short of grasping the distinctive differences that make superficial similarities fit into strikingly different patterns when placed in their larger contexts.

Take first the issue of personalism. Moroccans – indeed Arabs generally – do not regard the array of qualities and attachments by which others are known as abstract features that might be analyzed, in the manner of western philosophy and psychology, as discrete entities of a human being's composition. Rather they are aspects of social identity that mean something only as they cohere in a named individual. In every domain the attribution and assessment of others consists of a never-ending process of instantiation, of making the general comprehensible only as it is embodied in a concrete example. That is why, in forming social arrangements, one deals, as in the bazaar, by forging face-to-face bonds with another. That is why one constantly seeks knowledge of the particular contexts of another's associations. That is why stories move back and forth across time emphasizing contexts of relationship; why time itself is seen, not in terms of space or progression, but as clusters of obligation that define those involved in them; why, as one commentator put it, for the Arabs history is biography. A style exists that pervades much of Arab culture, one in which the individual unit is seen to exist within an overarching framework that is itself open-ended and unfinished. It is visible in Arab storytelling and music, where discrete units are built up over time and space rather than structured by fixed design. Words and concepts that frame relationships do not govern those relationships; they are a form of malleable framework by means of which negotiated, individual networks may be formed. The individual unit – of art, science, or society – is thus a momentary vessel for the features that have no other life than in their concrete embodiment.

So, too, in the law the stress on the individual as embodiment is central. From the earliest Islamic times men were seen as preeminently proprietors, defined by the associations formed with others through things. Contracts, therefore, were valid only when they took place face to face and involved simultaneous exchange, the action of each changing in that instant the network of obligations of both. Only the sacred Quran was treated differently for being written, though even it had to be committed to memory and repeated by chant. All else possessed its authority by being orally presented and orally attested, for only in that way could generalizable precepts be comprehended as incorporated in, having an effect on, and actually defining some individual. At least since the ninth century, when the main sources of law were established and the methods of reasoning were given authoritative shape, Islamic jurisprudence has stressed the responsibilities of each individual just as the Quran had settled the underlying moral precept when it stated that "no man bears the burden of another." The quest for knowledge by judges and their subalterns is a quest for the individuated; their inquiries represent a felt need to fix the individual before them in the web of concretized obligations that make them who they are and make association itself comprehensible. In

Islamic law the search for data about background and association is vital to the qadi's quest for a judgment that will avoid the chaos that hovers over society like a premonitory threat.

Reasoning, including legal reasoning, thus exemplifies this attempt to triangulate in on the individual by seeing the circumstances that comprise his social identity. In his questioning a judge will move through the various circumstances of background and past action to determine the unknown. His overall orientation is toward the consequences of individual acts and deeds. He seeks not an evaluation of the broad moral force of humanity's ways, but the concrete repercussions for his local community of personal utterances and acts that have entered the realm of the public. Like that overall framework that organizes but does not govern the Arab building, musical composition, or narrated tale, the qadi articulates the outer limits of the requisite and forbidden and, beyond that, seeks not the greater elaboration of governing precepts but, through the constantly individuated direction of the local, the lines of constancy and custom by means of which chaos may be avoided. His goal informs his method, his stress on the consequent his logic of analysis.

It is here, too, that what seems familiar in the Arab world is, in fact, not so easily equated with practice in the west. For if, as has been suggested, the goal of the qadi – his form of fact-finding and reasoning being marshaled accordingly – is to set people back on the course of negotiating their own arrangements without overstepping the limits of God, then the repercussions for this style of legal reasoning are quite distinct. The reference to collections of judicial practice and scholarly comment do not lead to the refinement of analytic concepts but to the maintenance of the distinctly local. A direct comparison to the two main systems of law and legal reasoning in the west – the Anglo-American common law system and the continental code systems – may help here. In the common law, as Edward Levi has convincingly argued, concepts are applied to concrete cases which in turn contribute to the formulation of the concepts themselves. If at first a category like "clear and present danger" is developed to conceptualize a form of political speech that may lead to rioting, in a subsequent case a judge may argue that the category applies only where no consitutional right of a higher order, like freedom of speech, could be undermined by the first heckler to threaten violence. A moving set of categorizing concepts thus gives shape to the common law mode of legal reasoning and allows for both regularity and malleability in the law. Continental systems, by contrast, start with elaborate codes whose lacunae are to be filled in by scholarly guidance or, failing that, by the judge acting as he thinks the legislator, given the opportunity, would have acted. The result is a body of scholarly literature that seeks to create doctrinal consistency similar to the organic integration of the code itself and judicial opinions that, far from showing how the present case fits with the facts and categorizing concepts of prior decisions, demonstrate the place of the particular case in the provisions of the code, its interpretation, or its spirit.

If Islamic law were like either of these systems we might, to choose an example that appears in collections of judicial practice, see a notion like the "friendship" of one who must be reimbursed for paying another's debts take its conceptual shape from a line of factually different cases or trace the legal meaning of "friendship" as it develops in scholarly treatises whose principal 'goal would be to demonstrate logical consistency with other concepts and provisions in the code. But Islamic law remains resolutely pragmatic and local. It does not seek to refine the concept involved or to make it an artifact in a neat system of codified categories. Rather, the concept retains its general shape and like other aspects of this system is projected, as it were, downwards: it is applied to situations to make their consequences comprehensible. It is not situations which are in service of conceptual elaboration. Just as human traits mean nothing unless attached to individual persons, the concept that is applied by the qadi must be filled in, indeed can only exist, through its individuated instance. The categories of Islamic legal thought, like those in other domains of this culture, are frameworks that delimit, not structures that govern.

Western commentators to this day therefore often make the mistake of characterizing Islamic law as poorly developed because they see in it none of that doctrinal refinement that would cast up large ideas like "good faith" or "negligence" and could, through the reasoning of the law, make of these ideas logically integrated propositions. But Islamic law is not undeveloped for lacking such an orientation. For Islamic law is as consistent and logical as any system in the west. The difference is that in Islamic law the concepts are measured against those cultural principles that allow people to return to the negotiation of their own arrangements. Its regularity is vertical, not horizontal: it seeks consistency with common-sense assumptions about humanity, not through the refinement of categories of its own creation. Islamic law is a system of adjudication, of ethics, and of logic that finds its touchstone not in the perfecting of doctrine but in the standards of everyday life, and measured in this way it is enormously developed, integrated, logical, and successful.

This quality of the qadi's legal reasoning, like his assessment of the facts, is not, as we shall see, unrelated to the religious and political implications of the law or to the vision of what is regarded as possible for any person or any judge to accomplish. For if it is true that in Morocco everyone, including judges in their official capacity, seeks information about others, it is also true that mankind is not regarded as capable of generating new moral concepts that would inform these relationships. Man's duty is to conform to God's moral limits, not to try to invent them. But within the limits of God one can create relationships and traffic in the knowledge of their existence, intricacies, and repercussions. The law cuts into this domain not to regulate the tenor of social creativity but, like religion, to reassert the terms that govern its outer limits. Islamic law does not, therefore, dictate the form every contract must take or develop an abstract concept of the contracts that could be applied to each instance. Instead, it specifies what contracts are impermissible because they adversely affect bargaining and allows local practice to govern all other instances. It does not prescribe the conditions involved in each marriage contract; it asserts the limits of the negotiable. Nor does the law attempt, through a concept like the public interest, to offer itself as a preferred vehicle for the reconstruction of society. Instead, it seeks to reestablish the grounds upon which local relationships can proceed notwithstanding certain inequalities that may result. It is, in short, a system that need not turn to that "artificial reason" Coke found so characteristic and so desirable in the political context of English law, however much it may be a system whose flexibility and responsiveness face severe tests in the climate of the modern nation-state. And it is to these political considerations, to the problem of the qadi's approach when he faces a case where law and fairness diverge, to the consequent vision of justice that emerges, and to the broader implications the work of his court suggests for a theory of judicial discretion that we must finally turn our attention.

4

Judicial discretion, state power, and the concept of justice

Some forty or so years ago Lord Justice Goddard of the English Court of Appeals, faced with a case in which the discretion of a lower-court judge could justifiably have led to either of two diametrically opposed results, remarked that "the court . . . is really put very much in the position of a Cadi under the palm tree. There are no principles on which he is directed to act. He has to do the best he can in the circumstances, having no rules of law to guide him." Lord Goddard's words were echoed a few years later by Justice Felix Frankfurter when he remarked that the United States Supreme Court is not a "tribunal unbounded by rules. We do not sit like a kadi under a tree dispensing justice according to considerations of individual expediency." As in so many other instances the image of the exotic has thus come to serve westerners as a standard against which we measure either our supposed advance along the enviable road of civilization or our felt loss for that state of nature or social harmony we imagine simpler societies have been able to retain.

Indeed, the image of the Islamic law judge, the qadi, is a particularly striking instance of the varying use of the exotic as mirror and as measure, for like many other such projections, the end to which the image has been put has changed as society and its forms of jurisprudence have changed. To Muslim artists stories like those contained in the eleventh-century *Maqamat* ("Assemblies") of al-Hariri provided ample opportunity to show qadis who were duped by clever litigants or hounded into personal generosity by the ceaseless squabbling of those who came before them. In comparison, to Europeans in the era preceding colonial instrusion the qadi was often seen quite positively as a model of the ideal magistrate, a man who bespoke the common standards and beliefs of his people with just that air of grace and wisdom, that dignity of attire, manner, and utterance that called forth visions of an Old Testament sage. By the nineteenth century, however, the image of the qadi had begun to shift away from that of a benign oracle of the community of believers to that of a judicial figure whose decisions, even if at times laudable and astute, were so unbounded as to appear arbitrary and even tyrannical. As western jurisprudence had shifted from a concern with natural law and its own romanticized projections of the natural justice of the folk to an emphasis on procedure, code, and appellate hierarchy, the image of the qadi had necessarily changed as well.

The qadi has thus become a key figure in contemporary scholarly debate. If earlier the qadi could serve western jurisprudence as the archetype for assessing the relation of law to communitarian values, he has come now to serve as a touchstone for measuring the relation between rules and principles on the one hand and the nature of judicial discretion on the other. For scholars and practitioners alike, the nature of qadi justice forms a challenge to our comprehension of the relations that exist – and even the relations that should be encouraged in any society to exist – among the state, the law, and the cultural concepts that inform their operation. For purposes of discussion it may prove helpful, therefore, to divide the question of qadi justice as a focus for analyzing these issues into three distinct parts. First, we need to consider the relation of the qadi's discretionary powers to the structure of the state. What is the connection among the sources of legitimacy by which his judgments gain authority, and to what extent do the ways in which he exercises them constitute a limitation or expansion of the power of the state or particular sectors of the society he serves? The second issue focuses more directly on the very nature of discretion. It asks what the relation is between rules of law, on the one hand, and principles, guidelines, and standards on the other. Can we, as a matter of logic and judicial policy, conceive of law in such a way as to demonstrate that there is no reason why any degree of judicial discretion need form a part of the adjudication process, and can we use the qadi, long seen as an extreme instance of such wide-ranging discretion, as a test for the debate over the legitimate and logical extent of such arbitrary power? And finally, as anthropologists looking at the fuller cultural context within which the qadi – and judges like him elsewhere – operate, can we specify how, in a sense, culture fills whatever discretionary space eludes either rules or principles, and thus pursue with some rigor that still elusive element that leads a judge to decide as he does?

First, then, there is the issue of the relation between qadi justice and the state. The terms for some aspects of this problem were, of course, set down by Max Weber when he chose the term *kadijustiz* to characterize that form of judicial legitimacy in which judges never refer to a settled group of norms or rules but are simply licensed to decide each case according to what they see as its individual merits. Weber was primarily concerned with the sources of legitimacy by which a specifically historical answer could be offered to the question, Why should the members of a given society do as those who possess authority direct them? He suggested that in patrimonial states like those found in the Middle East, where authority was legitimized by the traditions that had long given it credence, the law itself was unlikely to develop as an internally consistent body of rules because there was neither a separate commercial class nor a professional bar whose interests would be served by the creation of a law that could be administered by members of their own class. Indeed, Weber argued that in the absence of such a class acting as a political entity, it is unlikely that law can ever become a vehicle for the limitation of the powers of the state.

In fact, in both early times and modern, the relation between Islamic legal systems and the state is rather more subtle and complex than this paradigm would suggest. Since the earliest years of the Islamic era religious and legal scholars have elaborated a central distinction between what are called "the claims of God" and "the claims of man." Islam, with its heavily contractual image of the relation between God and man, its insistence that each man is responsible for his own actions, and its emphasis on the freedom of man to engage in negotiated arrangements that do not violate some clearly prescribed claim of Allah, encouraged exchange relationships of a highly personal nature. The law could enforce those aspects of human relationship that trenched on the prescriptions of God as contained in the Quran, but unlike the Old Testament or Roman Canon Law the number and extent of these divine claims on man are rather small. Instead, the ability to contract relationships was given considerable scope. Under the direction of Prophetic traditions, judicial analogies, and local practice the particular content of the law pertaining to these humanly created relationships was filled up with some specific content, but it was seldom that of rule-like prescriptions developed into an elaborate scheme. Rather, as we have seen, certain general precepts formed a conceptual framework that did not so much govern a host of relationships as fashion the broad terms by which they were conceived. So, for example, one often thinks of usury, which has generally been prohibited by all schools of Islamic law. But obtaining interest on loans, notwithstanding the fabrication over the years of a host of legal fictions through which it has been effectively made possible, really partakes of a broader concept of unjust enrichment of which usury was but one instance. Drawing on this broader category, Islamic law judges articulated general guidelines for particular issues, but instead of developing a logically consistent body of doctrine allowed local circumstance and individual instance to supply particular meaning and regularity to the concept in the locale under their jurisdiction.

What we have here, then, is a process that partakes of a set of deeper cultural features, all of which contribute to what has been called the cultural logic of dispute. One element is the belief that men are, at base, proprietary creatures. The Arabic term employed here is *mul*, a word that means much more than just "owner" or "proprietor": it also implies the idea that each man is a creature whose very identity is indissolubly linked to the relationships formed through exchange with others. The law supports this proprietary personality by giving preeminent stress to the bargained-for relationships among individuals. As a moral and religious entity the law does not seek to create the details of these identifying and sustaining relationships; rather it provides a context for the peaceable formation by individuals of their own ties under an institutional umbrella that, in theory, gives the force of government to the preservation of the rights of man assured by Allah.

Indeed, it is in this light that we can understand why, in the classical Islamic theory of the state, law and government were kept largely separate from one another. The state was seen not as an instrument for the application of law, nor were the courts, either through religious doctrine or a concept of the social good, envisioned as vehicles for economic redistribution or the construction of a particular political order. It was the duty of the political authorities to enforce the claims of God – even by maintaining their own courts for the punishment of specific crimes – but beyond that they were to insure that men could carry forth their own affairs without governmental interference. Legal authorities, through to the period of western influence, sought to protect the law – and their own positions – from encroachment by the state by, on the one hand, limiting the range of issues designated as claims of God and hence subject to the jurisdiction of a protective government and, on the other, by avoiding any attempt to make the rulers themselves subject to the direct power of the courts. By remaining resolutely focused on the individual the legal establishment forsook the politicization of the law; by avoiding inclusion of the law as an instrument of state policy the political authorities passed up the opportunity to use law as a vehicle of political centralization.

Given this orientation, the lack of doctrinal consistency and the particular scope of the qadi's discretion appear in a far more positive light. With its goal of maintaining the claims of men by setting litigants back on a course of negotiating their own relationships within the overall framework of a concept like unjust enrichment and an institutional structure that constantly leaves it to local personnel to shape the critical facts that can come before the qadi, the Islamic law courts developed neither mystifying procedures nor excessively arcane modes of reasoning to further their ends. It is often noted that the one thing courts must not seem to be is arbitrary, and Islamic law largely avoids this by pushing down to the level of the local the ascertaining of facts and their articulation in court. The common law courts of England could, to recall Sir Edward Coke's phrase, employ a specifically "artificial reason" in order to separate the courts further from the executive power of the state, and by thus mystifying the law various social groups, including the bench and the bar, could further the role of the law as a protection against state intrusion on their own proprietory interests. In Islamic law, by contrast, the courts have long operated not as a counterbalance to the state but as a stabilizing device among contending persons, an instrument by which the individual, within broad doctrines developed by the law, could seek the rough equivalence of an unimpeded bargaining stance through a court that helped to ensure this vision of the individual personality. A concept like unjust enrichment could, therefore, be used to keep individuals in a state of more or less equal bargaining status while presumptions in favor of the status quo could add stability to consequent relationships. As a result interest groups were hard put to use the law to any collective advantage that had not already been inscribed in local practice. And judges were, by the process of pushing all fact-finding and the shaping of issues down to the level of local practice, hard put, even if they were of such a disposition, to achieve the independent policy ends of some group or the state at large when so much turned on matters of local definition.

This is not to say that there were not conflicts between the state and the courts. It is true that, since early Islamic times, a clear jurisdictional division existed between those matters that could come before the qadi and those heard by political authorities – a caliph, a sultan, or a khalifa. And the range of discretionary punishments these officials could apply for certain infractions was also clearly established. Procedurally, too, the requirement of notarized documents or oral witnessing in the qadi's court was a far stricter requirement of proof than that used for criminal matters coming before a civil official, where a requirement of multiple witnesses would have made many convictions impossible. Sometimes the conflict between qadis and state officials was quite direct. State officials have at times tried to use the qadis to their own ends, and often one reads of instances like that of the medieval figure who was dissuaded by his travelling companion from accepting a post as qadi when the companions said to him, as perhaps someone should warn political appointees in our own society: "Are you not then aware that when Allah has no more use for a creature He casts him into the circle of officials?" Even in the primary locus of this study, the Moroccan city of Sefrou, stories are told of the time, around the turn of the century, when the local administrator tried to force the qadi to ratify land transfers that the administrator had coerced from local garden-owners. The qadi, with the encouragement of local religious figures, repeatedly refused to acquiesce. Some of the gardeners learned that the administrator was preparing to arrest the qadi, and they hurried to get the judge out of town in the dead of night. When the administrator discovered the qadi's absence the next day he rounded up the local religious scholars, tied them to one another with ropes around their necks, stuffed their mouths with hot peppers, and, after parading them around town, threw them in jail to starve to death. The next qadi, upon whom this lesson seems not to have been totally lost, signed the necessary documents. But the story has its characteristic twist. For qadis, though traditionally appointed by the sultan, were effectively subject to local approval. The locally important figures refused to accept the new qadi appointed by the administrator and sent a delegation to the sultan to inform him of the scholars' unjust demise. Their actions were sufficient to convince the sultan to remove the administrator for a period of enforced rethinking in the royal camp.

The nature of the entanglement changed in Arab countries like Morocco when they came under foreign colonization and again when they achieved national independence. The most significant alterations, to stick with the Moroccan case, were the adoption of national legal codes and the inclusion of the qadis' courts within a unified appellate judicial system operating under the central bureaucratic control of the Ministry of Justice. On the political level these changes have meant that judges are wholly dependent on the administrative hierarchy for advancement and placement and that should the government wish, it is in a much stronger position than ever to use the courts as an arm of executive policy. For reasons that will be discussed, however, this has not thus far proved to be the case.

Perhaps the single most important development in many of the new nations has been the adoption of national law codes. Morocco, like many other former colonial countries, has effectively adopted European codes for certain matters, but when the time came just after Independence to formulate a code of personal status that would govern most of the issues that come before the qadi, the approach taken was extremely conservative. Unlike their counterparts in Tunisia the Moroccan code-writers did not abolish all arbitrary divorce by husbands or effectively end polygamy nor did they, like some countries in the Arab east, take jurisdiction away from the local courts over many matters and place it in the hands of new national courts. The repercussions for the nature of judicial discretion have been intriguing. The code remains very close to traditional Malikite Islamic law. Indeeed, the draftsmen clearly state in a number of instances that where lacunae exist in the code judges should fill them in by reference to local custom, their own opinion, and the guidance offered by the body of judicial practice known as the ' amal. The result has been twofold. First, the code has preempted part of the qadi's former role. In the past, as we have seen, qadis and legal scholars set the general terms of discourse about legal matters – the broad criteria, the standards of generally acceptable arrangements, and a limited typology of acknowledged forms – while the process of incorporating local practice filled up much of the specific content of decisions. Now this broader role has been taken over in large part by the code: it decreases the role of the qadi as moral arbiter and standard-setter and thus opens the possibility for greater direct involvement in everyday affairs by the state. Moreover, the newly drafted code held out the possibility of encouraging renewed impetus to the formation of a body of contemporary judicial practice which might serve modern-day qadis as the earlier literature had served their predecessors. But here, too, there is little evidence of this happening. Instead, only a limited number of actual decisions has been compiled and communicated, and judges have no new source of law to rely upon in their decisions. This situation actually reinforces local decision making in one sense, for it continues the earlier belief that courts can justifiably reach different results as long as the reasoning process remains similar. What may, in the long run, temper this development is, however, the imposition of an appellate structure.

In classical Islamic thought no court could be higher than another because such a hierarchy would imply that the highest court actually knew the truth when in fact no such claim for absolute moral judgment is properly supportable. But bureaucracies have their own theology, and the appellate model imposed by the French was carried through to Independence times. The result, however, has not been the ubiquitous direction of substantive law by the higher courts or the reduction of the qadi's formal powers of independent judgment: few appellate decisions correct the qadi's approach in general terms so much as they emphasize one fact over another or remind the judge of a code provision he has missed. Thus appeals work less as a vehicle of political centralization or even as an instrument for creating national law and more as a sort of superior bureaucracy overseeing obvious abuses and lapses from a structure that retains considerable scope for local circumstance.

One other alteration affecting the nature of judicial discretion is the increased role of lawyers. Until recently most litigants in Islamic law courts have spoken for themselves or had a close relative act as their spokesman. This allowed for relatively low-cost litigation and for the qadi to make those personal assessments so characteristic of his mode of inquiry. In recent years, however, lawyers have increased considerably in number and effect. From the perspective of some qadis the presence of lawyers is desirable since lawyers can shape a case in more orderly fashion than contentious litigants. However, most judges still want to hear directly from the litigants and seek to use lawyers simply to help expedite the proceedings. The result, for the system as a whole, is an increase in the cost of litigation to clients but a certain amount of efficiency for the judges.

Moreover, popular attitudes about lawyers are not especially favorable. I had this brought home during my last trip to Morocco when my wife and I were looking for a place to live. We were discussing our needs over a glass of tea in the shop of a man who was a kind of local real estate broker. In the corner were seated two old men who were following our conversation carefully. Much of the discussion turned on the fact that it had been raining heavily in the region for many weeks, and unless the rains stopped very soon the entire grain crop for that year might be ruined. After a few moments the broker's son entered the shop. He remembered how, years earlier, I had been pointed out to him as the American in town. When he asked what I had been doing since my last visit to Sefrou I mentioned that, among other things, I had completed a degree in law. It was at this point that one of the two old men in the corner turned to the other and in a voice intended to be overheard by all said: "Six weeks of nothing but rain, and what does Allah bring us? Another lawyer!"

If lawyers increase the cost of litigation, it is not necessarily true – my aged humorist notwithstanding – that their presence leads, as is so often claimed, to social divisiveness or increased litigiousness. Quite aside from the fact that one seldom meets an American who has been involved in an actual lawsuit and almost no Moroccan who has not, court records suggest no sharp increase in recent years in the docket of the qadi's court when population is held constant. More intriguingly, it appears that, far from only exacerbating individual differences and contentiousness, the need to hire a lawyer to match one brought by the other side, has, by its increase in the costs of litigation, actually led many people to seek aid from kinsmen, neighbors, allies, and friends and thus reemphasizes, rather than disrupts, the need to retain certain bonds of social obligation and reciprocity.

It was, of course, Max Weber who not only posed some of the issues about judicial legitimacy and judicial discretion in terms of qadi justice but suggested that the social background and class interest of lawyers and judges – the people Weber called legal *honoratoires* – shaped the actual content of the judgments reached. It is true in Morocco, as in much of the Arab world, that those who seek a career on the bench, particularly as qadis, often come from traditional religious backgrounds and represent sectors of the society that see themselves as the guardians of a high tradition. But it is also true that education is one of the central avenues for advancement, and that since, as the Moroccan proverb says, "without the sons of the poor scholarship would die," many qadis come from poorer backgrounds and from smaller towns or rural areas. In Morocco, at least, it is hard to speak of judges representing one economic or regional group, though undoubtedly they are essentially conservative and religious – a factor that may well influence their perception of the litigants and situations that come before them. But that very background renders them something more than mere bureaucratic automata. For it also means that they have absorbed, in their education at mosque-universities like the Qarawiyin in Fez, that image of the qadi as a supervisor of social life and of the *shari'a* – the holy law – as an instrument for enforcing the claims of God even as it promotes the negotiated relations of men.

And it is this quality of legal goal and cultural context that brings us to the nub of judicial discretion not only in Sefrou or the Muslim world but as an issue that affects courts of law wherever they may be found. For if we are to approach judicial discretion neither as a black box whose qualities remain beyond eager academic grasp or tremulous political control nor as a feature of adjudication that must be eradicated in order for the rule of law to prevail, then we must look to the culturally characteristic factors that shape such discretion and the particular institutional history that informs its course.

In doing so we can reduce the scope of our own uncertainty about why and how judges decide as they do and, no less importantly, we can attend to the particular meaning for any given society of the special form of indeterminacy that will necessarily remain even when we have accounted for all else that bounds this exercise of power. So, to recapture these features as they relate to Islamic law, it appears that the central goal of the qadi is to put people back into a position of negotiating their own ties, within the bounds of the permissible, and that the entire process – of fact-finding and questioning, of using experts and legal presumptions – contributes to the reinforcement of the local in the context of the judicially cognizable. It means that the judge, even when applying a notion of public utility or distinguishing instances through the weighing of analogies, necessarily sets the terms of discussion in a rather conservative fashion and seeks to assure the status quo rather than reorganize relationships by judicial fiat. Indeed the legitimacy of the law lies in no small part in this aim. But such an interpretation also means that scholars who say that Islamic law lacks doctrinal rigor – that there is, for example, no idea of contract, only of particular forms of contract, or that doctrines of liability and excuse possess no ordering principles – miss the point that Islamic law is indeed highly consistent and refined but that it is so not by reference to its own developed doctrines but to the cultural assumptions about negotiated social ties. And we see this most clearly first when we look at those instances in which judges reach out to apply their own views even though the law might dictate a contrary result, secondly when we see this process working not only in an Islamic court but in a case drawn from the annals of American law, and finally when, as a result, we try to comprehend the ideas of justice that are thereby embraced.

Instances of a qadi deciding a case in a way that is clearly contradictory of the law are, of course, unusual. The result achieved may, as we have seen, be based on the imposition of a minority scholarly view in order to obtain a socially useful result. Alternatively the desired result may stem from the conflict posed to a broad moral and legal concept by a difficult factual situation. Consider, for example, the following two instances of unjust enrichment discussed in the literature on judicial practice:

In the course of concluding the marriage of his son a man fails to specify whether it will be he or his son who will be responsible for the payment of the bridewealth. Most commentors say that if at the time of the agreement the son had no resources of his own, the obligation falls on the father. But the position actually employed in most cases is that the burden rests on the son alone since, like a commercial transaction in which the sum owed is not a function of the resources one possessed at the time of the bargain, failure by the son to be liable would mean that he was unfairly obtaining something for which he is required to give nothing in exchange.

A similar situation is posed if a woman, who has agreed to pay her husband a sum of money in exchange for his divorcing her, later proves that in fact her husband had mistreated her and that she was, therefore, entitled to a judicial divorce without payment to the spouse. One view is that the obligation to pay must still be fulfilled, but judicial practice has led to the opinion that the woman was guaranteeing the payment of a sum to which the husband actually had no claim. From this perspective forcing her to pay him would therefore be tantamount to the unjust enrichment of the husband.

In each of these examples a judge has fashioned a way to avoid the clear implications of the predominant approach by couching his opinion in terms of unjust enrichment, a form of relationship which, though freely contracted, allows one person to consume the wealth of another without having subjected himself to any reciprocal claim. Each example supports the underlying principle that if people are to be encouraged to negotiate their own permissible arrangements the law must see to it that a real opportunity for bargaining exists. Contracts of adhesion, where the terms are not negotiable, or situations of unjust enrichment, where the imbalance precludes true give-and-take, will not receive judicial support. It is not the concept of unjust enrichment that now takes on theoretical development in the courts, nor is each new application of the phrase communicated and refined through successive cases. Rather, itemized instances may receive partial articulation in these terms with the appropriateness of application being a function of local consequence and judicial choice. Whether it is by specifying particular kinds of acceptable contracts or by setting the broad terms in which bargaining can go forward, Islamic law judges do not so much develop doctrine or encourage formalism as they oversee a process that is given specific content by local practice and individual negotiation.

A related set of considerations arises when the court is confronted with a situation in which the law, embodied now in the Code of Personal Status, clearly points in one direction but the qadi decides that strict application of the law would have an unfair effect in the particular case presented him. In one such instance the qadi of Sefrou was petitioned by a man in the army who asked either that his former wife relinquish custody of their child to him as required by the Code or move to his present posting so that he could oversee the child's upbringing. The wife answered that her former husband's life as a soldier would force her to move every few months. The court agreed with her and thereby clearly chose to look beyond the wording of the statute to its effect in this case. A similar instance could be cited of the qadi refusing to grant a husband who was in prison the right to recall his wife to his side even when the only form of divorce the qadi could by law grant her would have allowed this possibility. The reason for this decision, the qadi stated, was simply that the woman had already suffered enough from this man.

Through each of these instances the common point remains: the judge's discretion is at times clearly influenced by a sense of fairness that yields a result contrary to the clear letter of the law. At work, however, are not just the qadi's own values but an underlying concept of harm – an assessment, by no means predictable in result yet characteristic in mode, that considers the relative harm done by adherence to the law versus its lawful violation. And that assessment, in turn, will be deeply suffused by those cultural concepts that concern the character of human nature, the likely harm that may be done by persons of different backgrounds and character, and the sense of locally acceptable standards that will have been drawn within the ambit of the court's consideration by a process that constantly seeks to limit judicial arbitrariness by pressing issues into the mold of the conventions of the place.

Here we may be encountering one of those instances in which Moroccan society is changing so dramatically that both culture and law are being forced to respond. For as more people move from the areas where they were born, as more extended families dissolve into nuclear households, and as new bases for affiliation arise – occupational, professional, and political – the less confidently one can use features of background, quarter, tribe, or family as an index of character and harm. However, if the particular terms applied in this calculus of consequence may have changed, the underlying process seems unaltered, that of trying to ascertain, from social identity, an assessment of personal qualities and likely behavior. In the courts, as in the bazaar, the process is not without its subjective and variable elements. Like John Selden, the Muslim is well aware that "equity is a roguish thing," but because he sees its bounds as set by local practice, the form of judicial fact-finding, the precepts of social perception and Islamic morality he seldom finds the qadi's decisions fundamentally unacceptable.

But if it is true that local custom and local personnel are in fact central to the way judicial issues are shaped and decided, is it not still reasonable to suspect that particular interest groups have in fact molded the law and the courts to their own advantage? After all, do not the court personnel represent only a particular segment of society, and do not those who use the courts most often or most significantly possess influence beyond the normal course? The answer to this issue lies, I believe, in returning to a wider understanding of Moroccan society and its repercussions for the legal system.

Within Moroccan society at large power is enormously diffused. Individuals may build coalitions of allies in very different ways – using kinship, ethnicity, and economic contacts to forge alliances. But this must always be accomplished and maintained personally: social position alone is not enough to insure either regularized support or a perduring base from which to operate. Each point in the body politic – each individual – constitutes a locus for the development of power, and it is precisely because this flexibility is so highly valued that little support exists for the formation of common group identity expressed in the form of institutionalized power. Islamic law contributes to this pattern by its emphasis on the individual claimant, the individual case, and the individual's capacity to contract freely. Using concepts and procedures readily recognizable to all, the courts have not become the favored preserve of a limited number of people; lacking legislative functions they have not been subject to the cooptation of particular interest groups. And because the whole idea of a jural personality that is not an actual personality is absent, categories have not developed in the law favoring group representation. What has been said of the Saudi Arabians, and may also be said of Moroccans – that theirs is a world "in which people define tasks, roles, and institutions, not the other way around" – has led, in law as in society, to the relative absence of institutionalized group interests.

One feature of the legal culture that casts a particularly revealing light on this issue is the practice of corruption. It is, of course, very difficult to measure the extent of corruption in the courts of Morocco, but certain brute facts are undeniable. In Sefrou, for example, since independence one qadi has been dismissed for allegedly taking a bribe and another court official was disciplined for unauthorized use of government property. In both instances the officials were sent to rural posts but were soon back in favored positions, a pattern that is not uncommon in Moroccan official life. It is also quite clear that when land transfers are recorded with the court, sums of money often change hands to insure that reduced figures will be inscribed in order to avoid part of the tax due on the transactions. Common opinion holds that outright bribery is rare but hardly unknown, and one is left feeling simply that while the level of corruption is certainly not negligible it is also not such as would shock the conscience, say, of a Chicago alderman.

What is more interesting, however, is not just the extent of corruption but the form it takes, and it is here that the issue of group interest can be assessed. For there can be little doubt that corruption is practiced in a highly individual and case-by-case fashion. There are, at the level of the qadi's court, no cozy arrangements by which businessmen or elites can be assured that judges will do the "right" thing when matters of inheritance, or alimony, or notarized land documents are at issue. Instead, bribes involve individual cases and are similar in this respect to any other personal transaction.

Local practice, therefore, does not simply mean the practice of those who have captured the local court system, for power is too dispersed, the avoidance of institutionalized group interests too deep-seated, and the procedures of the law too decentralized to encourage a practice that is not found in other domains of social life. Men may continue to enjoy greater legal prerogatives than women, and Berber countrymen may encounter prejudice from urban Arab officials, but the predominant focus remains personalistic, and with it the range of persons and relevant customs remains remarkably diverse.

It is against this background that we can, therefore, begin to approach the issue of judicial discretion as a cultural phenomenon in its fullest possible context. It should, for instance, be possible to narrow the span of indeterminacy within which judicial discretion operates by comprehending the broader cultural circumstances and terms by which an issue is framed and addressed. Indeed, we should be able to approach not only foreign and exotic courts in these terms but those in western countries as well. A particularly good opportunity for comparing the cultural bases of judicial discretion is afforded by a famous case that arose some years ago in an American court of law.

On the afternoon of September 17, 1963, the well-known Washington attorney Edward Bennett Williams rushed into the office of Judge J. Skelly Wright of the U.S. Court of Appeals for the District of Columbia. As attorney for the Georgetown University Hospital he was seeking the approval of the court for a blood transfusion to be administered to Mrs. Jessie Jones, a patient in the hospital. Williams's request had been denied moments earlier by Judge Edward Tamm of the Federal District Court, so Williams hurried across the street to the appellate court and, finding Judge Wright the only member of the bench present, sought approval of his emergency request. The problem created by the case centered on the fact that Mrs. Jones, the 25-year-old mother of a seven-month old daughter, belonged to the Jehovah's Witnesses, a sect whose literal reading of the Old Testament prohibition against eating blood extends, even at the cost of one's life, to a medically prescribed transfusion. Mrs. Jones had been brought by her husband to the hospital's emergency room suffering from a ruptured ulcer that had already cost her two-thirds of her body's blood. With his clerk and Mr. Williams in tow Judge Wright hastened to the hospital. He spoke with Mrs. Jones's husband, himself a member of the sect, who refused permission for the transfusion but told Judge Wright that if the transfusion were ordered by the court the responsibility for that decision would not lie with him. Advised to obtain counsel immediately Mr. Jones placed a call to church officials and then returned to say that he did not want counsel. Judge Wright then asked the husband if he might see Mrs. Jones, a request which was immediately granted. Before going in, Judge Wright again spoke with the doctors, who said that without a transfusion the patient would surely die, and that even with the procedure her chances of survival were only 50–50. Entering the hospital room Judge Wright tried to communicate with the patient, but all he could make out were the words "against my will." Following unsuccessful pleas to the husband by the doctors and the Jesuit head of Georgetown University, Judge Wright signed an order allowing the transfusion to take place.

In writing up his opinion later, Judge Wright argued that the patient was not competent at the time to decide the issue of a transfusion, that the state should not allow a parent to abandon his or her child voluntarily, and that her having sought medical aid in the first place suggested that for Mrs. Jones death was, as Judge Wright put it, "not a religiously-commanded goal, but an unwanted side effect of a religious scruple." The judge said that by his act he was seeking to maintain the status quo and that he was doing so without sacrifice of the woman's religious beliefs. "I determined [he concluded] to act on the side of life." Three of Judge Wright's colleagues, however, disagreed with this opinion. Judge Miller said there were no adverse parties here – the patient herself was not even represented – and hence no legally cognizable case was presented, while Judge (later Chief Justice) Warren Burger argued that since the patient and her husband were willing to sign a document relieving the hospital of any liability, there simply was no basis for the court's intervention into the patient's private beliefs, beliefs which were entitled to judicial respect however much the court might feel them to be abnormal, unreasonable, or even absurd.

The *Georgetown* case thus presents a classic instance of the exercise of judicial discretion in the common law. Indeed it offers an opportunity to see how the very idea of judgment itself has been constituted in contemporary American culture. For Wright and his interlocutors are not simply engaged in a struggle over whether hospitals may require patients to submit to blood transfusions or whether the idea of attempted suicide applies to a conscientious believer refusing a life-saving procedure. Rather the courts are themselves partaking of the larger cultural discourse within which the issue of human judgment is itself cast, and when seen in the light of this continuing process the features that are at once distinctive to the law and characteristic of the culture in which it is embedded stand out with greater clarity.

Judge Wright and his detractors are both engaged in a dispute whose basic terms have changed significantly in the course of modern western history. The central question – How shall human judgment be understood and justified? – was, in the premodern period, largely framed in terms of inherited authority and divine sanction. Whether it was a father claiming the power to decide for his family, a king for his nation, or a judge for those arraigned before him, the discussions, whatever their particular results, necessarily included assertions framed by the categories associated with traditional legitimacy and supernatural validation. As in literature, theology, and family life, judgment and discretion in the law were seen largely in terms of social station and the order imposed by God.

These component categories were themselves fragmented by the changes wrought by seventeenth-century rationalism. Just as in society at large, where public and private life – whether economic, familial, sexual, or political – were becoming conceptually distinct, so, too, justice and its legal articulation were seen to reside in increasingly impersonal structures. The confrontation between King James and Sir Edward Coke exemplifies the moment at which these two conceptual orders were in contention: the King can still speak the language of divine right while Coke insists that law depends on an "artificial reason" linked not to station and nature but to profession and procedure.

But just as there had earlier been a strain of the irrational in western law and culture so, too, the idea of impersonal reason was opposed by the countervailing force of romanticism. For this is also the period in which the emphasis on individuality – indeed individualism – supported the proposition that insight into the truth may develop out of personal effort rather than from the qualities of dispassionate reason or impersonal profession. It was an image that fitted well with those who saw human judgment as a conjunction between one's self and ultimate truths just as the concept of judgment as disembodied Reason fitted well the rise of the bureaucratic state and the idea of law as a check on political power.

The confrontation between Judge Wright and his critics was to take place as between heirs to this conceptual history. Thus to his rationalist detractors the image of Judge Wright rushing out of the courthouse with his robes flapping is not just an example of unwarranted judicial activism but a flight from those abstract standards by which the exercise of human judgment may itself be justified. When, in remarks to his biographer, Wright says that "if I want to do something, I can find a way to do it," he suggests that juridical process may be secondary to desired results; when he goes further and says, "I try to do what's right," he implies that justice may not, in all instances, be consonant with law.

And when, of the *Georgetown* case itself, he later says that he believed this to be a matter that could not "be sliced up in neat legal categories," especially since "a life hung in the balance" with no time for "research and reflection," and that even years later it remains "hard to pinpoint reasons for making the decision," he places himself squarely in that cultural dialogue by which judgment itself is made comprehensible through the emphasis on an individual's own insight rather than the constraints imposed by impersonal standards. Wright himself may exemplify that viewpoint which suggests that to render judgment authentic an individual must at times rise above the confines of impersonality to grasp an essential truth. And his rejection of "neat legal categories" and strikingly personal finale ("I determined to act on the side of life") exemplify the modern version of the Romanticist approach to the issue of judicial discretion. But neither Warren Burger's countervailing quotation from Cardozo – "the judge . . . is not a knight-errant, roaming at will in pursuit of his own ideal of beauty or of goodness" – nor, indeed, his insistence on the limited power of judges to rectify society's ills makes sense except in terms of that same discourse by which, in a host of different domains, modern society has come to see judgment as composed by conscience and constraint, authenticity and impersonality, heroic achievement and collective wisdom.

The distinctive quality of contemporary American views of judicial discretion comes out even more sharply when compared to those that apply in the world of the qadi. For the categories by which Islamic culture and Islamic judges construct the nature of discretionary judgment differ significantly from those applied in the west. For both Judge Wright and his critics there is a fundamentally problematic aspect to the relation between law and ethics. Precisely how morality and legal propositions relate to one another forms the basis of innumerable works of philosophy and popular drama. This is not, however, an issue for the qadi. In Islam, law and morality are seen as entirely consonant, particularly inasmuch as law includes the local practice of the community and this "consensus" was acknowledged by the Prophet himself to be a legitimate source of law. Within the "limits of God" what the generality do is both morally acceptable and worthy of authoritative implementation. Similarly, it is part of the western discourse to raise the issue whether reason diminishes from one's essential humanity if it does not yield to a higher concern for mercy, fairness, or love, particularly when a human life is at stake. But for the qadi, reason – or perhaps more exactly, the process of reasoning – is the feature that is distinctive to human beings and to the preservation of society from chaos and strife. Religious ecstatics may seek unity with the supernatural through the suspension of their reason, but even they are not envisioned as being thus able to penetrate to a worldly sense of justice and equity, for that is the task reasoning man alone is capable of performing. And where both Judge Wright and his critics may carry on their discussion in terms of whether a judge may look beyond the law to the cultural standards or the "conscience of a sovereign people," for the qadi culture is not outside of the law but integral to it. For him it is not a question of how personalized the facts in a case should be – *whether* it is relevant that the Jehovah's Witness is a parent, at the doorstep of death, or comes from a religious family – and therefore whether the law needs to mask some features of the individual if it is to exercise judgment legitimately. On the contrary, to the qadi and his culture the "person" is always the subject – of law, or relationships, or political attachment – inasmuch as each individual embodies a set of features that may be readily deciphered through the configuration of concepts that define nature, background, and associations.

Problematic, too, in the west is whether wisdom is best achieved through means that are personal or impersonal – whether wisdom is a matter of insight and art or of science and the creation of normative criteria. By contrast, for the qadi no judgment is regarded as essentially superior to any other in the sense of being able to claim achievement of absolute truth, and hence the terms of discussion are both more relativized and more intensely personal. Stories are thus told of wise qadis who, suspecting a party to be untruthful, disguise themselves, embroil the other in some dishonest venture in the market-place, and then return to court to confront the individual with his true identity and personal appreciation of the other's character. It is not whether an individual qadi, in the quest of some authentic sense of himself, can penetrate to a truth beyond the social that is at issue: such a concept is simply absent from the approach to the problem of judgment found in the culture of the qadi. Rather, for him the issue is drawn in terms of that social truth which is lodged in the continuing assessment of others through cultural categories that span all domains of everyday life.

Thus what is problematic about human judgment in one culture is not an issue in the other. Wright and his critics may disagree as to whether the courts should be "result-oriented," but not so the qadis. For them what is problematic is the implication for social peace or chaos of those networks of affiliation that their judgments may affect, and thus the terms, as well as the differences of view, turn on the question of organizing the description of the situated person. By pressing this inquiry down into the hands of notaries, experts, witnesses, and oaths Islamic law has created a workable solution to the problem of uncertain human relationships, just as Wright and his colleagues avoid the open break their differences might engender by tacitly agreeing to share a common mode of expressing their processes of reasoning. Indeed, where American judges disagree over the issue of whether they are, in fact, ever exercising a wholly personal discretion, qadis – fearful that they may be exercising an impermissible interpretation of divine ordinance – see themselves as avoiding the risks this process might entail by drawing their judgments in the same social terms by which members of the culture at large make evaluations of others. For western judges and qadis alike the very nature of what is problematic for them and the terms that contribute to their way of reaching decisions are thus firmly embedded in the larger discourse of their respective cultures.

There is perhaps no place where a culture's approach to judgment and discretion comes more sharply to the fore than in the articulation of what it is that gives substance and meaning to its particular idea of justice. In a recent account of Islam in the modern world Malise Ruthven has written that:

> whereas Christianity is primarily the religion of love, Islam is above all the religion of justice. This does not, of course, mean that Christians are necessarily better at loving than Muslims, or that Muslim society lends itself more successfully to the realization of justice. . . Nevertheless. . . the two watchwords, love and justice, can usefully act as signposts to a wide range of differences between the two religions in terms both of their acknowledged practices and dogmas and of the unconscious prejudices of their adherents.

Everywhere one encounters in Islamic life the idea of justice: Respected figures are acknowledged for being just; relationships are valued when they partake of just arrangements; particular historical periods are admired because they were days when men acted justly. The Muslim concept of justice is thus one of those domains in which a host of social, political, and ethical ideas come into uneasy coalescence, and the contrast between American ideas, diverse, fluctuating, often inchoate, and Islamic ideas, challenged, hesitating, yet deeply sensed, is actually quite subtle. For if it is true that the present idea of justice in America overlaps with and incorporates ideas of equality (the law should be blind to social and biological differences) and ideas of autonomy (justice lies in the protection of my rights) then within the ambit of Islamic justice lie the central ideas of individuation (I must be seen as a whole person whose social traits contribute to a distinctive pattern) and the fair regulation of permissible exchange (the presentation of men's bargained-for claims within the limits set down by God). It is not rights that are at the center of Islamic justice, for no one expects rights to be recognized that are not granted by God or forcefully ensured by networks of obligation. Rather what is central is the process by which one's claims may be validated before the community in accord with local practice and the attestation of people who with their own eyes know what is so and will not risk their credibility as allies by refusing to say it.

It is particularly intriguing, in this respect, to mention to Moroccan judges that in western law it is considered only just that similar cases be decided similarly – a proposition that incorporates our vision of equality and its almost mathematical specificity – and then to ask whether a system like their own that involves no precedent or comparison with other cases does not violate justice. In my experience judges always reply with two arguments: The first thing to remember, say qadis, is that since no two individuals are exactly the same no two cases are precisely the same. Even the same individual committing the same act at a later date is changed by the fact that this is not the first instance of such behavior. But even more important, they say, is that if the mode of analysis and fact-finding is the same in each case although different judges may reach different conclusions, the results are equivalent because the process was identical. The logic of Moroccan jurisprudence thus seems to rest neither on the analytic philosopher's insistence on common definitions nor on a Wittgensteinian constancy of results, but on the settled process by which the locally known may be validly presented and authoritatively weighed. Small wonder, then, that a famous Moroccan poet of the sixteenth century, known as Mejdoub "the Sarcastic," should have put the matter so typically when he intoned that "if the times are just, one day is for me and one day is against me." And nowhere do those features that sound the common theme of justice in Moroccan thought come through more sharply than in a folktale told by the Berbers of the way in which justice and injustice became separate for all time.

At the beginning of time (goes the story) Justice and Injustice lived as neighbors. One day Injustice proposed that Justice join him in a pilgrimage to the shrine of a saint. "Prepare your provisions well," Injustice said, "for the voyage is a long one." On the assigned day the travelers set out. During the daylight hours they made their way and in the evening each prepared his own meal from his own provisions. Every evening, however, Injustice refrained from taking more than a few dates and a mouthful of water, and when Justice asked why he was not eating, Injustice simply replied that he was not very hungry. So it remained for the entire outward voyage.

On the return trip Justice found himself short of food. On the first evening, Injustice ate greedily from his store of honey and bread and meat and butter, offering nothing to his companion. Justice reproached him for acting so unworthily, but Injustice only laughed at the naïveté of his friend. After another day of long, hot travel, Justice again awaited some gesture on the part of his companion, but none was forthcoming. Noticing his friend's weakened condition Injustice said: "If you want to eat you must pay me, because I cannot feed you for nothing." "But I have nothing to give you," replied Justice; "I'll pay you when we arrive home." Injustice refused, saying, "You must pay me now since you want to eat now." Justice asked the price that he would have to pay in order to eat and Injustice replied: "You must give me one of your eyes." Justice's heart sank, but ultimately he decided to comply, reasoning that it was better for Justice to exist with only one eye than not to exist at all. The sentence was immediately executed. All the next day Justice stoutly resisted hunger and thirst, but by nightfall he could hold out no longer and ceded to Injustice his other eye in return for a bit of food. So it was that Justice became blind and wandered alone out into the desert.

Once again through this painful allegory we see those themes so characteristic of the concept of justice in this part of the world. For Justice is, like all creatures, responsible for his own actions and the consequences of them. His plight is deeply personalized; it is not an abstract idea that best conveys the qualities of a situation but the individuated, the contextualized, the personified. And although Injustice should so characteristically seek to bargain out his tie to Justice in wholly contractual terms, his unwillingness to partake of that hospitality and reciprocity so integral to proper relations gives sharp emphasis to the tradition of the Prophet that reminds the believer that "you can give an unjust law to a just judge, but you cannot give a just law to an unjust judge." It is ironic, too, that it should be Injustice who scrupulously adheres to the Islamic prohibition against contracts for future performance and goes on to insist that failure to pay for something when it is given would constitute a form of unjust enrichment. Is it for placing law over fairness that Injustice is to be condemned? Is it for agreeing to an unbargainable contract that Justice is submitted to suffering? Or is it because where Islamic law is absent and the appeal to conscience over public force that it embraces is lacking one must expect even Justice to argue, as a writer from quite a different tradition once put it, that "nothing is real to us but hunger, nothing sacred save our own desire"? In this moral tale, in the application of the qadi's discretionary judgment, in the validation by one witness of the just and equitable qualities of another, and in the Quranic admonition that "no man bears the burden of another" the Islamic sense of justice and injustice thus finds its characteristic voice.

In their own distinctive ways folktales and legal cases both explore the boundaries of the concepts and relationships by which a people tests its own standards of power and of fairness. In many developing nations – as well as many western countries – dissatisfaction with the delay and cost of adjudication has, however, led to the introduction of new courts whose jurisdiction overlaps or supersedes that of existing courts. Whether it be the People's Court of China, Cuba, or the National Broadcasting Corporation, these alternative forums reveal much about the acceptable limits of judicial authority and discretion. In 1974, following the model of Iran, Morocco instituted a series of local courts in which nonappealable decisions on minor cases, heard by a judge chosen from among the members of a local nominating body, were to be made without reference to any particular body of law. To many these courts represented a return to the arbitrary decisions of political officials who once held jurisdiction over matters not clearly within the aegis of the qadi's court. Where proponents argued that the courts would be close to the people by applying local custom, detractors saw in these courts a complete absence of legal principles and insufficient procedural regularities to guard against abuse. Observing their proceedings in the late 1970s one could not help but be struck with the rapidity of judgment, the political dependence of the judge, and the hostility with which many people approached the court proceedings.

The eventual failure of these courts thus attests, in Morocco as in other Muslim countries, to the deep-seated fear not that particular powerful individuals may be able to use a court to their personal advantage but that if the forum does not draw local circumstance in through the processes that have long characterized the courts of the qadi – especially for matters traditionally within the power of the *shari'a* to decide – the absence of legitimacy for the alternative system will threaten society as a whole with unjust times. Whatever the future may hold for Islamic law – an increase in its criminal law dimensions as the state uses religion to help in its monopolization of violence, a reinforcement of the classical period's use of independent reasoning as a bridge toward unavoidable change – it is very probable that the legitimacy of local *shari'a* courts everywhere will, as in Morocco, depend in no small part on their capacity to acknowledge and incorporate local practice within a mode of reasoning and procedure that carries reverberations from and to a number of other domains of social life.

Other and still deeper forces may, however, be at work in a number of Middle Eastern cultures, forces that span the bounds of law and society affecting different domains in ways that escape easy prediction. I do not mean the opposition between what westerners are wont to call modernism and fundamentalism, with its connotations of appellate judges in westernized robes versus the chief executioner lopping off hands or heads in the public market-place. Rather what is implied is a potential shift in some of the most fundamental terms by which the discussion of law, no less than other social issues, goes forward. In Morocco, as in some other Muslim countries, an intriguing alteration may, therefore, be underway in several of the central concepts with which this study has been concerned.

It may be, for example, that for the first time a concept of probability is finding its way into the conceptual framework of Moroccan life. In the past people always spoke of events as either occurring or not: good harvests happened or they did not, allies remained faithful or they did not, the times were just or they were not. Terms like *imken* or *warra bemma*, often translated as "maybe" or "might," fit a conceptual scheme of positive and negative, not of true probability. But just as in the west, where the introduction of the idea of statistical probability in the seventeenth century had profound reper- cussions for literature, theology, and science no less than for law, so, too, in Morocco terms that were previously connected only with occurrence/nonoccurrence now bear overtones of the possibility of increasing the chances for one or another result. In agriculture people speak of what can be done to increase the frequency of positive outcomes rather than just saying that three or four years of every seven are favorable. In politics they speak of how to maximize outcomes within a given frequency. And in law, the qadis are also speaking about the likelihood of various results and calculating consequences in terms of the probability of achieving one or another outcome.

Similarly, the idea of causality may be undergoing change. As we have seen, it has commonly been assumed in Moroccan culture that human or divine agency lies behind all events. To know how something happened you mainly need to know who made it happen. Even a complex series of events was perceived and retold in terms of the actor involved at each stage. Now, however, one sees instances in which chains of events are themselves seen to entail their own natural or probable consequences. Once set in motion, a political election, a familial dispute, or an economic venture may be spoken of as incorporating forces that work their way without constant human intervention. In the courts, this means that circumstantial evidence, rather than evidence of character, of persons-in-context, becomes more acceptable. Just as elaborated rules of evidence did not develop in the common law until the eighteenth century, when the idea of probability had taken its place in the common sense of society, so, too, in the Muslim Middle East causality in the law may undergo significant alteration as the idea of human agency itself becomes increasingly problematic.

Two other linked concepts may also be following suit. Intentionality, as we have seen, has been envisioned as directly inferable from overt acts, words, and background indicators. From the science of physiognomy to the use of expert advice the courts, like ordinary individuals contemplating a new dyadic bond, arranged their view of another's intended meaning in the belief that mental processes were indeed accessible and hence subject to influence. But as physical mobility has increased and ties of family, craft, and residence become unlinked the ability to infer mind from context has become more uncertain. This may be contributing, even in "fundamentalist" Islamic thought, to a greater emphasis on strict liability and to an assessment of intent as either irrelevant or in need of professionalized measures of evaluation. So, too, for the idea of responsibility. For if events at times take a course of their own, if others' minds become dimmer to view, and if events may be varied in their likelihood of occurrence, then may not a person's capacity for responsible action – so central to the whole moral vision of Islam and the categories by which the Sacred Law has been enforced – become a contingent factor rather than the stable referent it has long been? If so, the repercussions in the law, as in society, may be vast and unforeseeable.

That the people of the Muslim world may be in the process not of a new round of events played by the old rules but of rethinking the categories of their own reality is a prospect of endless fascination and uncertainty. Whatever its course and implications one thing is reasonably clear: the courts of the qadi will continue to constitute a forum in which those terms will be reflected and from which they will, in part, be shaped, for it is in that realm – so open to the contention of people and their culture – that a portion of that future will be made visible to those caught up in its uncertain course.

I began this chapter by citing something once said by Mr. Justice Frankfurter. In drawing to a close it is perhaps fitting to quote something once said by Mrs. Felix Frankfurter. Following one of his public speeches an enthusiast once asked Marion Frankfurter if she did not think the Justice to be a marvelous speaker. "Yes," replied Mrs. Frankfurter, "though as a lecturer he does have two faults. The first is that he always strays from his main point, and the second is that he always manages to wander back to it!"

In the study of law and anthropology, it may be argued, such meandering is actually more of a virtue than a detriment. For it is by moving back and forth across the analytic line that separates law from culture that we can perhaps best see how problems raised in each domain find their response not within their own confines alone but within the ambit of both – how the determination of facts depends on the concepts by which mind and act are categorized in ordinary discourse, or how the conceptual framework of legitimate authority is shaped by its judicial articulation. Seen from this perspective our questions about both law and society become more capacious and intriguing. We can ask not just how people use rules to limit action but why they employ the very form of legal rules to accomplish this end. Thus, in the context of Islamic justice our study of Moroccan courts may suggest more generally that although in Arab society one cannot create relationships from whole cloth or ever ignore that premonitory fear of chaos writ deep in religious doctrine and the common view of humanity, one can indeed traffic in the knowledge of others' obligations and seek thereby to contain their intricacies and repercussions. In a world where institutions take a backseat to personalities, where the assessment of situations turns on the evaluation of social features only as they have taken shape in a given individual, and where this personal instantiation necessarily makes the reduction of relationships to simple rules or roles patently adverse to each man's need to contract ties freely where best he can, the law works less to regulate the details of relations than to establish the parameters of the permissible. Islamic law thus seeks neither to equalize wherever inequality exists nor to offer a preferred terrain for the reconstruction of society through judicial legislation. Rather, it seeks to reestablish the grounds upon which negotiation can proceed with whatever inequalities of circumstance may locally prevail. The weakness of such a system may be an incapacity to generate change by restructuring the distribution of resources or the rules by which they may be adduced or applied. But by drawing culture into the law and law into the culture Islamic law may have allowed that process of bargaining out relationships – in all its stolid variety and tremulous solidity – to retain its characteristic form and vitality for such an extraordinarily long time. That indeterminacy of which Sally Falk Moore has spoken, in which people struggle to limit their situations by the fixity of their relationships or to exploit the ambiguities of convention to fabricate more favorable contexts of engagement, often finds in the law an instrument – as profound as religion, as persuasive as material want – through which an image of oneself and one's society may be most forcefully presented.

And where – whether in the Arab world or in our own – the law has come to be a central forum in which concepts and relationships reveal themselves most openly, one will find a judge who must ultimately decide the issue at hand. The struggle for the heart and mind of such a judge will take quite different forms and lead to markedly different institutional constraints and repercussions. But through the characteristic manner of their decisions and through our own attempt to comprehend them the actions and judgments of qadis and of judges afford an unusual opportunity to see a culture enact a vision of itself and of its deepest aspirations.

Notes and Bibliography

The following notes are intended both as references for specific arguments and quotations in the text and as a selective guide to readers on the relevant literature. References are keyed to the pages in the main text in order to avoid the distraction of numerous specific footnotes.

The Bibliography contains a fuller set of references than those mentioned in the notes. Titles have been selected both as a guide to more specialized reading and as an indication of the context within which many of the issues raised in this study must be placed.

Notes

1 Law and culture: the appeal to analogy

p. 2   The fullest statements of the realist position remain Karl Llewellyn, *Jurisprudence: Realism in Theory and Practice* (Chicago: University of Chicago Press, 1962), and Jerome Frank, *Law and the Modern Mind* (New York: Brentano's, 1930). The best work in the positivist tradition is H. L. A. Hart, *The Concept of Law* (Oxford: Clarendon Press, 1961). The relation of law to the political and economic order has come under close scrutiny by members of the Critical Legal Studies school, whose work is well represented in "Critical Legal Studies Symposium," *Stanford Law Review*, vol. 36, nos. 1 and 2 (January 1984), and Roberto Ungar, *The Critical Legal Studies Movement* (Cambridge, Massachusetts: Harvard University Press, 1986). See also Duncan Kennedy and Karl E. Klare, "A Bibliography of Critical Legal Studies," *Yale Law Journal*, vol. 94, no. 2 (December, 1984), 461–90.

p. 2   The quotation comes from Benjamin N. Cardozo, *The Nature of the Judicial Process* (New Haven: Yale University Press, 1921), p. 10.

p. 3   Butler's statement occurs in the section of his *Notebooks*, 2 entitled "Music, Pictures and Books: Thought and Word."

p. 3   Although his biographers are not explicit on the issue, I think it is very likely that Lewis Henry Morgan, the man in whose honor the lecture series on which this book is based, himself drew on analogies from the law for his understanding of anthropological issues. Morgan tried, for example, to conceive of Iroquois organization as having similarities to the construction of a legal corporation and sought to express the forms of kinship behavior in terms similar to jural rules. His use of analogies drawn from the law illustrates both the strengths and weaknesses of such an approach, revealing the common principles that inform kinship and polity but encouraging a view of social organization that stresses formal closure over processual refashioning. On Morgan's work and life, see Carl Resek, *Lewis Henry Morgan: American Scholar* (Chicago: University of Chicago Press, 1960); on the relation of law and metaphor generally, see James Boyd White, *The Legal Imagination* (Boston: Little, Brown, 1973; abridged edition, University of Chicago Press, 1985).

pp. 4–5   A list of major works in the field of anthropology and law is beyond the scope of this book, but at the risk of considerable underinclusion the following may be noted as among the recent works that have proved most stimulating in constructing the present argument: Elizabeth Colson, *Tradition and Contract* (Chicago: Aldine Press, 1974); John L. Comaroff and Simon Roberts, *Rules and Processes: The Cultural Logic of Dispute in an African Context* (Chicago: University of Chicago Press, 1981); Lloyd A. Fallers, *Law Without Precedent: Legal Ideas in Action in the Courts of Colonial Busoga* (Chicago: University of Chicago Press, 1969); Max Gluckman, *The Ideas in Bratose Jurisprudence* (New Haven: Yale University Press, 1965); Ian Hamnett (ed.), *Social Anthropology and Law* (New York: Academic Press, 1977); Karl N. Llewellyn and E. Adamson Hoebel), *The Cheyenne Way* (Norman: University of Oklahoma Press, 1941); Sally Falk Moore, *Law as Process: An Anthropological Approach* (London: Routledge and Kegan Paul, 1978); Stuart A. Schlegel, *Tiruray Justice* (Berkeley: University of California Press, 1970).

Among the seminal works discussing the analysis of culture that have influenced this study are: Kenneth Burke, *The Philosophy of Literary Form* (New York: Vintage Books, 1957); Clifford Geertz, *The Interpretation of Cultures* (New York: Basic Books, 1973); Suzanne Langer, *Philosophy in a New Key* (Cambridge, Massachusetts: Harvard University Press, 1942); Leonard B. Meyer, *Music, The Arts, and Ideas* (Chicago: The University of Chicago Press, 1967); Walker Percy, *The Message in the Bottle* (New York: Farrar, Strauss, and Giroux, 1976); and David Schneider, *American Kinship: A Cultural Account*, 2nd edition (Chicago: University of Chicago Press, 1980).

p. 6   The work in the Sefrou area has thus far yielded the following main books: Clifford Geertz, Hildred Geertz, and Lawrence Rosen, *Meaning and Order in Moroccan Society* (New York: Cambridge University Press, 1979); Clifford Geertz, *Islam Observed* (New Haven: Yale University Press, 1968), and *Local Knowledge* (New York: Basic Books, 1983); Paul Rabinow, *Reflections on Fieldwork in Morocco* (Berkeley: University of California Press, 1977); and *Symbolic Domination: Cultural Form and Historical Change in Morocco* (Chicago: University of Chicago Press, 1975); and Lawrence Rosen, *Bargaining for Reality: The Construction of Social Relations in a Muslim Community* (Chicago: University of Chicago Press, 1984).

p. 6   Although the literature on Islamic legal history and doctrine is extensive, there are very few studies of the actual operation of contemporary courts of law anywhere in the Arabic-speaking world, a fact that makes direct comparison between my own observations of the Islamic courts of Morocco and those of other places extremely difficult.

Among the most useful discussions of modern Islamic court proceedings are: Richard T. Antoun, "The Islamic Court, the Islamic Judge, and the Accommodation of Traditions: A Jordanian Case Study," *International Journal of Middle East Studies*, 12 (1980), 456–67; Judith Djamour, *The Muslim Matrimonial Court in Singapore* (London: Athlone Press, 1966); Carolyn Fluehr-Lobban, *Islamic Law and Society in the Sudan* (London: Frank Cass, 1987); Enid Hill, *Mahkama! Studies in the Egyptian Legal System* (London: Ithaca Press, 1979); Brinkley Messick, "Legal Documents and the Concept of 'Restricted Literacy,'" *International Journal of the Sociology of Language*, 4 (1983), 41–52, and his "Prosecution in Yemen: The Introduction of the Niyaba," *International*

Journal of Middle East Studies, 15 (1983), 507–18; Ann E. Mayer (ed.), *Property, Social Structure and Law in the Modern Middle East* (Albany: State University of New York Press, 1985); and June Starr, *Dispute and Settlement in Rural Turkey* (Leiden: E. J. Brill, 1978). Two older but still very useful descriptions of Islamic court proceedings will be found in the books by John H. Wigmore, *A Kaleidoscope of Justice* (Washington, DC: Washington Law Book Co., 1941), pp. 217–58; and *A Panorama of the World's Legal Systems* (Washington, DC: Washington Law Book Co., 1936), pp. 531–650d.

p. 11   The argument summarized here is elaborated in my *Bargaining for Reality: The Construction of Social Relations in a Muslim Community*. The semantic history of many of the Islamic concepts discussed here is analyzed in Toshihiko Izutsu, *Ethico-Religious Concepts of the Qur'an* (Montreal: McGill University Press, 1966); and *God and Man in the Koran* (Tokyo: Keio Institute of Cultural and Linguistic Studies, 1964).

p. 12   The transcription of Arabic used here is based on that of the most generally accessible Arabic–English dictionary, Hans Wehr's *Dictionary of Modern Written Arabic*, ed. J. Milton Cowan (Ithaca: Cornell University Press, 1976), with some modifications for the Moroccan colloquial dialect.

p. 13   The Conrad quotation comes from *An Outcast of the Islands* (London: Penguin, 1976 [orig. pub. 1896]), p. 113.

p. 15   The "milky way of instants" phrase appears in Louis Massignon, "Le Temps dans la pensée islamique," *Eranos-Jahrbuch 1951*, 20 (1952), 141. For a discussion of Moroccan concepts of time, history, and narrative style see my *Bargaining for Reality: The Construction of Social Relations in a Muslim Community*, pp. 165–79.

p. 15   The lines quoted are from Katherine Slater Gittes, "*The Canterbury Tales* and the Arabic Frame Tradition," *P.M.L.A.* (*Publications of the Modern Languages Association*), 98 (1983), 243–44.

pp. 16–17   Most of the literature on Islamic law is concerned with doctrine rather than actual legal decisions. The best overview of Islamic legal doctrine remains Joseph Schacht, *An Introduction to Islamic Law* (Oxford: Clarendon Press, 1964), while excellent material, particularly pertinent to the North African situation, is contained in Louis Milliot, *Introduction à l'étude du droit musulman* (Paris: Recueil Sirey, 1953).

The Malikite school of Islamic law practiced in Morocco does not differ radically from other orthodox schools, although it does tend more than others to stress the intentions of contracting parties, a feature that can be seen in such sources as the English translation of Imam Malik, *Al-Muwatta* (Norwich: Diwan Press, 1982); F. H. Ruxton, *Maliki Law* (London: Luzac, 1916); and a modern compendium referring to various schools, ʿAbdur Rahman I. Doi, *Shariʿah: The Islamic Law* (London: Ta Ha Publishers, 1984). On the history and modern reform of Islamic law there are two particularly useful studies: Noel Coulson, *A History of Islamic Law* (Edinburgh: Edinburgh University Press, 1964); and Norman Anderson, *Law Reform in the Muslim World* (London: Athlone Press, 1976). Of particular relevance to this study is the title essay in Geertz's *Local Knowledge*, which compares the relation of law and culture in Morocco and Indonesia.

Actual legal decisions, especially below the highest court level, are not regularly reported in most Arab countries, and therefore it is difficult to analyze and compare judicial practice. Some Moroccan cases do appear in the *Revue algérienne, tunisienne, et marocaine de legislation et de jurisprudence*, the *Revue marocaine de droit*, and the *Revue juridique, politique et économique du Maroc*. Undoubtedly the richest collections of case decisions are those edited by Louis Milliot, *Recueil de jurisprudence chérifienne*, of which volumes I and II appeared in 1920, volume III in 1924 (all published in Paris by Editions Leroux), and volume IV, jointly edited with J. Lapanne-Joinville, in 1952 (Paris: Librairie Recueil Sirey, 1952). A full translation of a representative case from the Milliot collection appears in Wigmore, *A Panorama of the World's Legal Systems*, pp. 593–614. For examples from the law of torts, see Emile Tyan, *Le Système de résponsabilité délictuelle en droit musulman* (Beirut: Imprimerie Catholique, 1926).

None of the cases from the qadi's court of Sefrou is published. With the aid of an assistant who deciphered and orally translated each dossier from literary to colloquial Arabic with me, some 400 cases – only a few of which can be discussed in detail in this work – were collected from the court records. The citation system used here is the same employed by the court, with the year in which litigation began followed by the docket number of the case.

2   Determining the interminable

p. 21   The quotation about evidence is from R. C. van Caenegem, *The Birth of the English Common Law* (Cambridge: Cambridge University Press, 1973), p. 62.

p. 22   The role of lies is not precisely the same throughout the Arab world. See, for example, the Lebanese situation described in Michael Gilsenan, "Lying, Honor, and Contradiction," in Bruce Kapferer (ed.), *Transaction and Meaning* (Philadelphia: Institute for the Study of Human Issues, 1976), pp. 191–219. For a fuller discussion of the Moroccan instance, see my *Bargaining for Reality: The Construction of Social Relations in a Muslim Community*, pp. 117–33.

p. 23   The role of notaries and forms of witness proof are more fully described in my "Equity and Discretion in a Modern Islamic Legal System," *Law and Society Review*, vol. 15, no. 2 (1980–81), 217–45. The seminal work on legal fictions remains Ian Fuller, *Legal Fictions* (Stanford: Stanford University Press, 1967).

pp. 23–24 Islamic judges are not surprised by people lying in court if an oath has not yet been taken, a situation that recalls the analysis of some countries of sub-Saharan Africa in Lloyd A. Fallers, "Customary Law in the New African States," *Law and Contemporary Problems*, vol. 27, no. 4 (Autumn 1962), 605–16, at 608. The local reaction to the 1967 Middle East war is described in my "A Moroccan Jewish Community during the Middle East Crisis," *American Scholar*, 37 (1968), 435–51.

On the role of documents see Jeanette A. Wakin, *The Function of Documents in Islamic Law* (Albany: State University of New York Press, 1972); and Brinkley Messick, "Literacy and the Law: Documents and

Document Specialists in Yemen," in Daisy Hilse Dwyer (ed.), *Law and Islam in the Middle East* (South Hadley, Massachusetts: Bergen, 1988).

p. 27 The story of Potiphar's wife appears in the Quran at Sura 12, verses 23–29, and in the Old Testament at Genesis 39.

p. 30 The High Court opinion on experts will be found in *Recueil des arrêts de la Cour suprême, Chambre civile 1957–62* (Rabat: 1968), Case no. 102, pp. 186–87. The Court has also repeatedly held that it has no right to substitute its own discretion for that of a lower court unless a clearly articulated standard has been violated. See *ibid.*, case nos. 2, 110, 123, 135, 140, 166, and 176.

pp. 31–32 The importance and procedure of oath-taking in various Islamic jurisdictions and historic periods are described in Robert Brunschvig, "Le Système de la preuve en droit musulman," *Recueil de la Société Jean Bodin pour l'histoire comparative des institutions, La Preuve*, 18 (1963), 177–80; Almenouar Kellal, "Le Serment en droit musulman, école malékite," *Revue algérienne, tunisienne et marocaine de législation et de jurisprudence*, 74 (1958), 18ff.; and Herbert J. Liebesny, *The Law of the Near and Middle East: Readings, Cases, and Materials* (Albany: State University of New York Press, 1975), pp. 243–54.

p. 32 The quotation from the Ohio court appears in the case of *Clinton* v. *State, Ohio State Reports*, vol. 33 (1877) at p. 33. For an interesting discussion of the modern rationale for the oath in the United States, see Richard O. Lempert and Stephen A. Saltzburg, *A Modern Approach to Evidence* (St. Paul: West Publishing Co., 1977), pp. 334–35.

p. 33 The Italian version of the decisory oath is cited and analyzed in G. L. Certoma, *The Italian Legal System* (London: Butterworth, 1985), p. 204.

p. 33 The quotation about the *muddaʿi* and *muddaʿa ʿalay-hi* comes from the commentary of al-Sharnubi as translated and analyzed in Alexander D. Russell and Abdullah Al-Maʾmun Suhrawardy, *First Steps in Muslim Jurisprudence* (London: Luzac, 1906), p. 99. On the role of presumptions generally in Moroccan law see J. Lapanne-Joinville, "Etudes de droit musulman malékite: les présomptions," *Revue algérienne, tunisienne et marocaine de législation et de jurisprudence*, 73 (1957), 99–113.

p. 34 An interesting example of the presumptions at work in a child custody case will be found in Milliot and Lapanne-Joinville (eds.), *Recueil de jurisprudence cherifienne*, vol. IV, pp. 129–35. Other instructive cases on the order of oath-taking appear in the same collection at pp. 61–67 and 253–55, as well as in vol. III at pp. 113–16.

On the interplay of rational and irrational elements in oaths and ordeals in various legal systems, see Rebecca V. Colman, "Reason and Unreason in Early Medieval Law," *Journal of Interdisciplinary History*, vol. 4, no. 4 (Spring 1974), 571–91; and William A. Shack, "Collective Oath: Compurgation in Anglo-Saxon England and African States," *Archives européenes de sociologie*, 20 (1979), 1–18.

The major work containing Tylor's ideas is his *Primitive Culture* (London: John Murray, 1871), while Frazer's views are most fully developed in *The Golden Bough* (London: Macmillan, 1890). On Malinowski's thought in this regard see his *A Scientific Theory of Culture and Other Essays* (Oxford: Oxford University Press, 1960). The more recent approach described here derives from Suzanne Langer, *Philosophy in a New Key* (Cambridge, Massachusetts: Harvard University Press, 1942), and the analyses of social life as performative events developed by Victor Turner, *The Ritual Process* (London: Routledge and Kegan Paul, 1969), and *From Ritual to Theatre* (New York: Performing Arts Journal Publications, 1982). The umpire joke is related by Hadley Cantril, "Perception and Interpersonal Relations," in Alfred E. Kuenzli (ed.), *The Phenomenological Problem* (New York: Harper, 1959) p. 198.

3 Reason, intent, and the logic of consequence

p. 39 A published version of Coke's response to King James appears in Sir Edward Coke, *The First Part of the Institutes of the Lawes of England* (London, 1628), s. 138 at 97b.

p. 41 In the vast literature on the sources of Islamic law Joseph Schacht's *Origins of Muhammadan Jurisprudence* (Oxford: Oxford University Press, 1950) still remains preeminent. Muhammad Ibn Idris al-Shafiʿi was the eighth-century commentator most responsible for establishing the sources of Islamic law, and a translation and analysis of his work will be found in Majid Khadduri, *Islamic Jurisprudence: Shafiʿi's Risala* (Baltimore: Johns Hopkins University Press, 1961).

p. 43 Milliot's collections, *Recueil de jurisprudence chérifienne*, contain numerous examples of judicial reasoning in terms of "positive" and "negative" assertions. Among the most instructive are the cases that will be found in volume I at pp. 107–24; volume II at pp. 17–32, 133, 167–68; and volume IV at pp. 110–14 and 349–59.

p. 44 The case that presumes usury to be the norm in financial transactions with Jews appears in Milliot, *Recueil de jurisprudence chérifienne*, vol. II, pp. 88–92, while the case of the presumptively lying administrator is reported in the same volume at pp. 190–215.

pp. 46–47 The quotation about *fatwas* is from Brinkley Messick, "The Mufti, the Text and the World: Legal Interpretation in Yemen," *Man* (New Series), 21 (1986), 111. The existence of the ʿ*amal* literature was first brought to western attention by Louis Milliot in his *Démembrements du Habous* (Paris: Editions Leroux, 1918), pp. 13–21, and later elaborated in his *Recueil de jurisprudence chérifienne*, vol. I, pp. 14–21 and vol. IV, pp. v–xix. Where Milliot saw the collections of judicial practice as forming a body of positive law, Jacques Berque, in his *Essai sur la méthode juridique Maghrébine* (Rabat, 1944), suggested that the literature functioned in much the same way as case law in western systems. For a critique and reevaluation of both positions see my "Islamic 'Case Law' and the Logic of Consequence," in Jane Collier and June Starr (eds.), *History and Power in the Study of Law* (Ithaca: Cornell University Press, 1989). A translation and analysis of one of the leading collections of Moroccan ʿ*amal*, that of Sijilmasi, is contained in Henry Toledano, *Judicial Practice and Family Law in Morocco* (Boulder and New York: Social Science Monographs and Columbia University Press, 1981).

p. 48 The 1946 case is reported in Volume IV of Milliot's *Recueil de jurisprudence chérifienne*, pp. 339–45. For an interesting discussion of the relation between law and urban design in the Middle East see Malise Ruthven, *Islam in the World* (London: Penguin, 1984), pp. 176–79.

p. 50   The case of a wife initiating divorce appears in Toledano, *Judicial Practice and Family Law in Morocco*, p. 128; the case of the birth costs is case no. 65/137 (joined with case no. 64/365), which was filed in the qadi's court of Sefrou in 1964.

p. 50   John Dewey's argument appears in his "Logical Method and Law," *Cornell Law Quarterly*, 10 (1924), 17–27. The quotation about a judge's duty to avoid civil strife is from Sidi ʿ Isa al-Sijistani's *Nawazil* as cited in Toledano, *Judicial Practice and Family Law in Morocco*, p. 167.

p. 51   The issue of intentionality in Moroccan society and law is discussed in comparison to western examples in my "Intentionality and the Concept of the Person," in J. Roland Pennock and John W. Chapman (eds.), *Criminal Justice* (NOMOS XXVII) (New York: New York University Press, 1985), pp. 52–77; and *Bargaining for Reality: The Construction of Social Relations in a Muslim Community*, pp. 47–56. Among the most useful sources for an understanding of the Islamic law of homicide are: J. N. D. Anderson, *The Maliki Law of Homicide* (Zaria, Nigeria: Gaskiya Corp., 1959); Jacques el-Hakim, *Le Dommage de source Délictuelle en droit Musulman* (Paris: Librairie Générale de Droit et de Jurisprudence, R. Pichon et R. Durand-Auzias, 1964); and Edward Westermarck, "Customs Connected with Homicide in Morocco," *Transactions of the Westermarck Society*, 1 (1947), 7–38. On the related issue of responsibility, see my "Responsibility and Compensatory Justice in Arab Culture and Law," in Ben Lee and Greg Urban (eds.), *Semiotics, Self, and Society*.

       For a fascinating fictional example of the role of intent in a Moroccan setting, see the story entitled "The Eye" in Paul Bowles, *Midnight Mass* (Santa Barbara: Black Sparrow Press, 1981), pp. 151–62.

p. 51   The warning against adjudication contrary to the judicial practice was made by Sidi Isa al-Sijistani in his *Nawazil*, as quoted in Toledano, *Judicial Practice and Family Law in Morocco*, p. 167.

pp. 51–52   The interpretation of the tradition about hiding one's sins comes from Ahmad Zaki Yamani, *Islamic Law and Contemporary Issues* (Jidda: The Saudi Publishing House, 1968), while the tradition itself is elaborated in Th. W. Juynboll, "Adhab," in H. A. R. Gibb and J. H. Kramers (eds.), *Shorter Encyclopaedia of Islam* (Leiden: E. J. Brill, 1961), pp. 15–16.

p. 52   The comment by the Saudi Arabian scholar, Sheikh Abdulla Qadir Shaybat al-Hamd of Medina Islamic University, is quoted with approval by Sheikh Saleh Ibn Mohammad al-Laheidan, a member of the Council of the Supreme Court of Saudi Arabia, in an article entitled "Means of Evidence in Islamic Law," in *The Effects of Islamic Legislation on Crime Prevention in Saudi Arabia, Proceedings of the Symposium Held in Riyadh, 16–21 Shawal 1396 [9–13 October 1976]* (Rome: United Nations Social Defense Research Institute [for the Ministry of Interior, Kingdom of Saudi Arabia], 1976), pp. 150–92, at p. 164. Al-Laheidan himself goes on to say (p. 171): "The judge, being endowed with this exceptional ability [to make accurate guesses], can follow the procedural steps which force a person to make his own confession." On the relation of criminal law and intent in the Hanifi school of Islamic law, see A. Ibrahim Pacha, *De la responsabilité pénale en droit islamique d'après la doctrine hanafite* (Paris: T.E.P.A.C., 1944).

p. 53   For a case interpreting the intent of a trust, see Milliot, *Recueil de jurisprudence chérifienne*, vol. II, pp. 167–68. The example of friendship appears in Toledano, *Judicial Practice and Family Law in Morocco*, p. 45.

p. 54   The relation of individual units to encompassing frameworks is discussed in a most interesting way by Katherine Slater Gittes, "The *Canterbury Tales* and the Arabic Frame Tradition." Among the best analyses of historical Islamic contract law are: Babar Johansen, "Sacred and Religious Element in Hanafite Law – Function and Limits of the Absolute Character of Government Authority," in Ernest Gellner, *et al.* (eds.), *Islam et politique au maghreb* (Paris: Editions du Centre National de la Recherche Scientifique, 1981), pp. 281–303; Nabil A. Saleh, *Unlawful Gain and Legitimate Profit in Islam* (Cambridge: Cambridge University Press, 1986); and A. Udovitch, "Islamic Law and the Social Context of Exchange in the Medieval Middle East," *History and Anthropology*, 1 (1985), 445–65.

p. 54   The passage from the Quran is at Sura 35, verse 18.

p. 55   Levi's seminal work is *An Introduction to Legal Reasoning* (Chicago: University of Chicago Press, 1948). For a general introduction to continental legal reasoning, see John Henry Merryman, *The Civil Law Tradition* (Stanford: Stanford University Press, 1969).

p. 56   On the absence of concepts like good faith in Islamic law see Schacht, *An Introduction to Islamic Law*, p. 397; and his "Islamic Religious Law," in Joseph Schacht and C. E. Bosworth (eds.), *The Legacy of Islam*, 2nd edition (Oxford; Clarendon Press, 1974), pp. 396–97. For a provocative argument that contracts in the west should be understood not as isolated agreements but as complex and continuing interrelations, see Ian Macneil, "Relational Contract: What We Do and Do Not Know," *Wisconsin Law Review*, vol. 1985, no. 3 (1985), 483–525.

4   Judicial discretion, State power, and the concept of justice

p. 58   Justice Goddard's remarks appear in *Metropolitan Properties Co. Ltd. v. Purdy, All England Reports*, vol. 2 (1940), p. 188; those of Justice Frankfurter in *Terminiello v. Chicago, United States Reports*, vol. 337 (1949), p. 11. Other common law case references to qadi justice will be found in John Makdisi, "Legal Logic and Equity in Islamic Law," *American Journal of Comparative Law*, vol. 33, no. 1 (1985), 63–92. For an eighteenth-century example of a positive western view of a qadi see Anquetil Duperron, *Législation orientale* (Amsterdam: Marc-Michel Rey, 1778), pp. 1–13, 94–95, and 246–47.

pp. 59–60 Max Weber's discussion is developed in *Max Weber on Law in Economy and Society* (New York: Simon and Schuster, 1967), especially at pp. 213ff. There is also a useful discussion of Weber's views on Islamic law in Bryan S. Turner, *Weber and Islam: A Critical Study* (London: Routledge and Kegan Paul, 1974), pp. 107–21.

pp. 60–61 The "cultural logic of dispute" phrase comes from the subtitle to John. L. Comaroff and Simon Roberts, *Rules and Processes: The Cultural Logic of Dispute in an African Context* (Chicago: University of Chicago Press, 1981). The idea of the proprietary person as it has been developed in a school of Islamic legal thought which, in this instance, is not unlike that of Morocco, is discussed by Babar Johansen, who also says, apropos the relation of the state to the individual: "The state as the guardian of the *huquq allah* [the claims of God] necessarily partakes of the absolute character of the [claims of God]. It is, then, true that the Hanafite law did not develop any 'overt institutions for the plural and democratic settlement of the humdrum, non-absolute issues of daily policy.' But this is not due to any '*gout d'absolu*,' it is rather due to the preoccupation of the lawyers [i.e., legal scholars] with the humdrum, non-absolute issues of daily life. It is the lawyer's preference for the *huquq al-ʿibad* [the claims of man] which determines their understanding of the absolute prerogative of the state. At the same time, this understanding implies the criterion by which a good government can be judged. It is not 'total rectitude' which is expected from the government. The government has to safeguard the [claims of man]. The absolute character of government action is only accepted as long as it secures the settlement of the humdrum, non-absolute issues of daily life by the individual legal persons." Babar Johansen, "Sacred and Religious Element in Hanafite Law – Function and Limits of the Absolute Character of Government Authority," in Ernest Gellner, *et al.* (eds.), *Islam et politique au maghreb* (Paris: Editions du Centre National de la Recherche Scientifique, 1981), p. 303.

p. 62   The lines quoted appear in Noel Coulson, "Doctrine and Practice in Islamic Law," *Bulletin of the School of Oriental and African Studies*, 18 (1956), 212. On the criminal punishments available to state officials, see Schacht, *An Introduction to Islamic Law*, pp. 175–87.

p. 63   The 1958 Code of Personal Status (*Mudawwana*) is available in the Arabic text, together with an occasionally misleading French translation, in André Colomer, *Droit musulman*, 2 vols. (Rabat: Editions La Porte, 1963 and 1967), and is updated in his "Législation comparée: Maroc," *Juris-Classeur de droit comparé* (Paris: Editions Techniques, S.A., 1985). Portions of the Code also appear in English in Tahir Mahmood, *Family Law Reform in the Muslim World* (Bombay: N. M. Tripathi Pvt. Ltd., 1972). For analyses of the 1958 Code, see also J. N. D. Anderson, "Reforms in Family Law in Morocco," *Journal of African Law*, 2 (1958), 146–59; Maurice Borrmans, *Statut personnel et famille au maghreb de 1940 à nos jours* (Paris: Mouton, 1977); and Charles Gallagher, "New Laws for Old: The Moroccan Code of Personal Status," *American Universities Field Staff Reports, North Africa Series 1* (Hanover, N.H.: American Universities Field Staff, 1959).

pp. 63–64   On the absence of appellate courts in Islam, see Martin Shapiro, *Courts: A Comparative and Political Analysis* (Chicago: University of Chicago Press, 1981), pp. 194–222. Among many Berber tribes of North Africa there did, however, exist an appellate structure for the decision of cases according to Berber customary law.

p. 65   Weber's discussion of legal *honoratoires* is in *Max Weber on Law in Economy and Society*, pp. 198–223. The intellectual background and training of a Moroccan judge is described in Dale F. Eickelman, *Knowledge and Power in Morocco: The Education of a Twentieth-Century Notable* (Princeton: Princeton University Press, 1985), while legal education in classical Islamic institutions is discussed in George Makdisi, *The Rise of Colleges: Institutions of Learning in Islam and the West* (Edinburgh: Edinburgh University Press, 1981).

p. 66   The case of the son paying a bridewealth contracted by his father appears in Toledano, *Judicial Practice and Family Law in Morocco*, p. 44; that of the woman who need not have paid her husband for a divorce at pp. 44–45.

p. 67   The case of child custody involving the soldier husband is Sefrou qadi's court, case no. 1962/279. The case of the imprisoned husband, Sefrou qadi's court, case no. 1961/262, is reported in full in my "Equity and Discretion in a Modern Islamic Legal System," 235–37. The quote about Saudi Arabians is from Peter A. Iseman, "The Arabian Ethos," *Harper's Magazine*, 256 (February 1978), 50.

pp. 69–73   The Jehovah's Witness case is *Application of the President and Directors of Georgetown College, Inc., Federal Reporter, Second Series*, vol. 331, pp. 1,000–1,018, decided by the Federal Court of Appeals for the District of Columbia in 1964. The comments by Judge Wright in subsequent years, as well as Professor Bickel's reactions, appear in Arthur Selwyn Miller, *A "Capacity for Outrage": The Judicial Odyssey of J. Skelly Wright* (Westport, Connecticut: Greenwood Press, 1984), pp. 174–88.

p. 74   Ruthven's remarks are from his *Islam in the World*, pp. 227–28.

pp. 74–75   The emphasis on contradictory judicial results being understood as linked by common procedures is emphasized by Berque, *Essai sur la méthode juridique maghrébine*, p. 21, and further supported by Safia K. Mohsen, "Islam: The Legal Dimension," in Don Peretz, Richard U. Moench, and Safia K. Mohsen, *Islam: Legacy of the Past, Challenge of the Future* (Croton-on-Hudson, N.Y.: North River Press, 1984), pp. 99–128.

pp. 74–75   Mejdoub's comment about just times appears in J. Scelles-Millie and B. Khelifa, *Les Quatrains de Medjdoub le Sarcastique: poète maghrébine du XVIe siècle* (Paris: G.-P. Maisonneuve at Larose, 1966). The Berber story about justice exists in a French translation from the Berber by Moha Souag entitled "La Justice et l'Injustice," *Lamalif*, no. 83 (October 1976), 41. On the philosophical concept of justice in Muslim thought, see Majid Khadduri, *The Islamic Concept of Justice* (Baltimore: Johns Hopkins University Press, 1984). The remark about hunger is by Okakura Kakuzo, *The Book of Tea* (Rutland, Vermont: Charles E. Tuttle, 1956).

p. 79   Sally Falk Moore offers a very striking analysis of indeterminacy in social life in her *Law as Process*, pp. 32–53.

Bibliography

Afchar, Hassan. 1973. Equity in Musulman Law. In Ralph A. Newman (ed.), *Equity in the World's Legal Systems*. Brussels: Etablissements Emile Bruylant. Pp. 111–23

al-Wancharisi, Ahmad. 1909. Portrait du parfait qāḍī. In *La Pierre de touche des fetwas: choix de consultations juridiques des faqih du maghreb*, tome III, Archives Marocaines 13

Anderson, J. N. D. [Sir Norman]. 1951. Homicide in Islamic Law. *Bulletin of the School of Oriental and African Studies*, **13**, 811–28

1958. Reforms in Family Law in Morocco. *Journal of African Law*, **2**, 146–59

1959. *The Maliki Law of Homicide*. Zaria, Nigeria: Gaskiya Corp.

1976. *Law Reform in the Muslim World*. London: Athlone Press

Antoun, Richard T. 1980. The Islamic Court, the Islamic Judge, and the Accommodation of Traditions: A Jordanian Case Study. *International Journal of Middle East Studies*, **12**, 456–67

ʿAwwa, Muhammad Salim. 1982. *Punishment in Islamic Law: A Comparative Study*. Indianapolis: American Trust Publications

Azad, Ghulam Murtaza. 1985. Conduct and Qualities of a Qāḍī. *Islamic Studies*, **24**, 1, 51–61

Bassiouni, M. Cherif (ed.). 1982. *The Islamic Criminal Justice System*. New York: Oceana Publications

Belaid, Sadok. 1973. *Essai sur le pouvoir créature et normatif du juge*. Tunis: Publications de l'Université de Tunis

Berman, Harold J. 1968. Legal Reasoning. *International Encyclopedia of the Social Sciences*, vol. 9. New York: Macmillan and the Free Press. Pp. 198–99

Berque, Jacques. 1944. *Essai sur la méthode juridique maghrébine*. Rabat

1953. Problèmes initiaux de la sociologie juridique en Afrique du Nord. *Studia Islamica*, **1**, 137–62

1967. L'Ambiguité dans le fiqh. In Jean-Paul Charnay (ed.), *L'Ambivalence dans la culture arabe*. Paris: Editions Anthropos. Pp. 232–52

1982. *Ulémas, fondateurs, insurgés du Maghreb: XVIIe siècle*. Paris: Sinbad

Borrmans, Maurice. 1977. *Statut personnel et famillie au maghreb de 1940 à nos jours*. Paris: Mouton

Bousquet, G.-H. 1949. Le Chameau volé: document de procédure marocaine. *Hespéris* **36**, 431–38

Bowles, Paul. 1981. *Midnight Mass*. Santa Barbara: Black Sparrow Press

Brunschvig, Robert. 1963. Le Système de la preuve en droit musulman. *Recueil de la Société Jean Bodin pour l'histoire comparative des institutions, La Preuve*, **18**, 169–86

Burke, Kenneth. 1957. *The Philosophy of Literary Form.* New York: Vintage Books

Butler, Samuel. 1917. Music, Pictures and Books: Thought and Word, *Notebooks*, 2. New York: Dutton. Pp. 93–109

Caenegem, R. C. van. 1973. *The Birth of the English Common Law.* Cambridge: Cambridge University Press

Cantril, Hadley. 1959. Perception and Interpersonal Relations. In Alfred E. Kuenzli (ed.), *The Phenomenological Problem.* New York: Harper

Cardozo, Benjamin N. 1921. *The Nature of the Judicial Process.* New Haven: Yale University Press

Certoma, G. L. 1985. *The Italian Legal System.* London: Butterworths

Chehata, Chafik. 1966. L'Equité en tant que source du droit hanafite. *Studia Islamica*, **25**, 123–38

Chelhod, Joseph. 1971. *Le Droit dans la société bédouine.* Paris: Librairie Marcel Rivière et Cie

Chenery, Thomas (trans.). 1867. *The Assemblies of Al Hariri*, vol. I. London: Williams and Norgate

Christelow, Allan. 1985. *Muslim Law Courts and the French Colonial State in Algeria.* Princeton: Princeton University Press

Cleveland State Law Review. 1985–1986. Conference on Comparative Links Between Islamic Law and the Common Law. *Cleveland State Law Review*, **34**, 1–144

Coke, Sir Edward. 1628. *The First Part of the Institutes of the Lawes of England.* London: Societie of Stationers

Colman, Rebecca V. 1974. Reason and Unreason in Early Medieval Law. *Journal of Interdisciplinary History*, **4**, 4 (Spring), 571–91

Colomer, André. 1963. *Droit musulman, tome premier: Les Personnes – La famille.* Rabat: Editions La Porte

1967. *Droit musulman, tombe deuxième: Statut successoral.* Rabat: Editions La Porte

1985. Législation comparée: Maroc. *Juris-Classeur de droit comparé.* Paris: Editions Techniques, S.A.

Colson, Elizabeth. 1974. *Tradition and Contract.* Chicago: Aldine Press

Comaroff, John L. and Simon Roberts. 1981. *Rules and Processes: The Cultural Logic of Dispute in an African Context.* Chicago: University of Chicago Press

Conrad, Joseph. 1976. *An Outcast of the Islands.* London: Penguin [orig. pub. 1896]

Coulson, Noel. 1956. Doctrine and Practice in Islamic Law. *Bulletin of the School of Oriental and African Studies*, **18**, 211–26

1964. *A History of Islamic Law.* Edinburgh: Edinburgh University Press

Court of Appeals of Great Britain. 1940. *Metropolitan Properties Co. Ltd. v. Purdy.* All England Reports 2: 188

Critical Legal Studies Symposium. 1984. *Stanford Law Review.* **36**, 1 and 2 (January)

Davis, Kenneth Culp. 1971. *Discretionary Justice.* Urbana: University of Illinois Press

Deprez, Jean. 1981. Pérennité de l'Islam dans l'ordre juridique au Maghreb. In Ernest Gellner, et al. (eds.), *Islam et politique au maghreb.* Paris: Editions du Centre National de la Recherche Scientifique. Pp. 315–53

Dewey, John. 1924. Logical Method and Law. *Cornell Law Quarterly* **10**, 17–27

Djamour, Judith. 1966. *The Muslim Matrimonial Court in Singapore.* London: Athlone Press

Doi, ʿAbdur Rahman I. 1984. *Shariʿah: The Islamic Law.* London: Ta Ha Publishers

Doualibi, Marouf. 1941. *La Jurisprudence dans le droit islamique.* Paris: G.-P. Maisonneuve

Dulout, F. 1947. Le Serment dans le droit musulman et les coutumes. *Revue algérienne, tunisienne et marocain de legislation et de jurisprudence,* part I, 1–31
Duperron, Anquetil. 1778. *Législation orientale.* Amsterdam: Marc-Michel Rey
Dworkin, Ronald. 1985. *A Matter of Principle.* Cambridge, Massachusetts: Harvard University Press
Dwyer, Daisy Hilse. 1982. Litigants law and judicial tensions in Morocco: Westermarck's ethnography of law in a contemporary context. In Timothy Stroup (ed.), *Edward Westermarck: Essays on His Life and Works.* Helsinki: Acta Philosophica Fennica. Pp. 260–73
Eickelman, Dale F. 1985. *Knowledge and Power in Morocco: The Education of a Twentieth-Century Notable.* Princeton: Princeton University Press
El Fassi, Allal. 1977. *Défense de la loi islamique.* Charles Samara, translator. Casablanca: Imprimerie Eddar El Beida
el-Hakim, Jacques. 1964. *Le Dommage de source délictuelle en droit musulman.* Paris: Librairie Générale de Droit et de Jurisprudence, R. Pichon et R. Durand-Auzias
Essaid, Mohamed Jalal. 1971. *La Présomption d'innocence.* Rabat: Editions La Porte
Fallers, Lloyd A. 1962. Customary Law in the New African States. *Law and Contemporary Problems,* **27,** 4 (Autumn), 605–16
    1969. *Law Without Precedent: Legal Ideas in Action in the Courts of Colonial Busoga.* Chicago: University of Chicago Press
Farago, John M. 1980. Intractable cases: The role of uncertainty in the concept of law. *New York University Law Review,* **55,** 195–239
Federal Court of Appeals for the District of Columbia. 1964. Application of the President and Directors of Georgetown College, Inc. Federal Reporter, Second Series, v. 331. Pp. 1000–1018
Fluehr-Lobban, Carolyn. 1987. *Islamic Law and Society in the Sudan.* London: Frank Cass
Frank, Jerome. 1930. *Law and the Modern Mind.* New York: Brentano's
Frazer, Sir George. 1890. *The Golden Bough.* London: Macmillan
Fuller, Ian. 1967. *Legal Fictions.* Stanford: Stanford University Press
Gallagher, Charles. 1959. New Laws for Old: The Moroccan Code of Personal Status. *American Universities Field Staff Reports, North African Series 1.* Hanover, N.H.: American Universities Field Staff
Geertz, Clifford. 1968. *Islam Observed.* New Haven: Yale University Press
    1973. *The Interpretation of Cultures.* New York: Basic Books
    1983. Local Knowledge: Fact and Law in Comparative Perspective. In his *Local Knowledge.* New York: Basic Books. Pp. 167–234
Geertz, Clifford, Hildred Geertz, and Lawrence Rosen. 1979. *Meaning and Order in Moroccan Society.* New York: Cambridge University Press
Gilsenan, Michael. 1976. Lying, Honor, and Contradiction. In Bruce Kapferer (ed.), *Transaction and Meaning.* Philadelphia: Institute for the Study of Human Issues. Pp. 191–219
Gittes, Katherine Slater. 1983. The *Canterbury Tales* and the Arabic Frame Tradition. *P.M.L.A. (Publications of the Modern Languages Association),* **98,** 243–44
Gluckman, Max. 1965. *The Ideas in Barotse Jurisprudence.* New Haven: Yale University Press
Gottheil, R. J. H. 1908. The cadi, the history of this institution. *Revue des études ethnographiques et sociologiques,* **1,** 385–93
Grabar, Oleg. 1984. *The Illustrations of the Maqamat.* Chicago: University of Chicago Press

Greenawalt, Kent. 1975. Discretion and Judicial Decision: The Elusive Quest for the Fetters that Bind Judges. *Columbia Law Review*, **75**, **2**, 359–99

Guay, F. and M. Ben Daoud. 1933. Le Mariage dans la jurisprudence des cadis de Fès (' Amal Al-Fâsî). *Revue algérienne, tunisienne et marocaine de legislation et de jurisprudence*, 49e année, juin-juillet, 178–84 and août–septembre, 185–207

Guiraud, A. 1925. *Jurisprudence et procédure musulmanes*. Casablanca: Imprimerie du Petit Marocain

Hallaq, Wael B. 1984. Was the gate of ijtihad closed? *International Journal of Middle East Studies*, **16**, **1**, 3–41

Hamnett, Ian (ed.). 1977. *Social Anthropology and Law*. New York: Academic Press

Hardy, M. J. L. 1963. *Blood Feuds and the Payment of Blood Money in the Middle East*. Leiden: E. J. Brill

Hart, H. L. A. 1951. The Ascription of Responsibility and Rights. In Anthony Flew (ed.), *Logic and Language* (First Series). Oxford: Blackwell. Pp. 145–66

1961. *The Concept of Law*. Oxford: Clarendon Press

Hill, Enid. 1978. Comparative and Historical Study of Modern Middle Eastern Law. *American Journal of Comparative Law*, **26**, **2**, 279–304

1979. *Mahkama! Studies in the Egyptian Legal System*. London: Ithaca Press

Hopkins, J. F. P. 1958. *Medieval Muslim Government in Barbary*. London: Luzac

Ibn Duyan, Ibrahim ibn Muhammad ibn Salim. 1961. *Crime and Punishment under Hanbali Law*. Cairo. Translated by George M. Baroody

Iseman, Peter A. 1978. The Arabian Ethos. *Harpers*, **256** (February), 50ff.

Izutsu, Toshihiko. 1964. *God and Man in the Koran*. Tokyo: Keio Institute of Cultural and Linguistic Studies

1966. *Ethico-Religious Concepts of the Qur'an*. Montreal: McGill University Press

Johansen, Babar. 1981. Sacred and Religious Element in Hanafite Law – Function and Limits of the Absolute Character of Government Authority. In Ernest Gellner, et al. (eds.), *Islam et politique au Maghreb*. Paris: Editions du Centre National de la Recherche Scientifique. Pp. 281–303

Juynboll, Th. W. 1961. Adhab. In H. A. R. Gibb and J. H. Kramers (eds.), *Shorter Encyclopaedia of Islam*. Leiden: E. J. Brill. Pp. 15–16

Kakuzo, Okakura. 1956. *The Book of Tea*. Rutland, Vermont: Charles E. Tuttle

Kassem, Hammond. 1972. The Idea of Justice in Islamic Philosphy. *Diogenes*, no. 79, 81–108

Kellal, Almenouar. 1958. Le Serment en droit musulman, école malékite. *Revue algérienne, tunisienne et marocaine de législation et de jurisprudence*, **74**, **1**, 18–53

Kennedy, Duncan and Karl E. Klare. 1984. A Bibliography of Critical Legal Studies. *Yale Law Journal*, **94**, **2** (December), 461–90

Kerr, Malcolm H. 1968. Moral and Legal Judgment Independent of Revelation. *Philosophy East and West*, **18**, **4**, 277–83

Khadduri, Majid. 1961. *Islamic Jurisprudence: Shafi'i's Risala*. Baltimore: Johns Hopkins University Press

1984. *The Islamic Concept of Justice*. Baltimore: Johns Hopkins University Press

Khattibi, Mustapha. 1969. Le Rôle de la cour suprême marocaine. *Revue juridique et politique d'outre-mer*, **23**, 999–1003

Lane, (Edward. 1889. *The Thousand and One Nights*. London: Chatto and Windus

Langer, Suzanne 1942. Philosophy in a New Key. Cambridge, Massachusetts: Harvard University Press

Lapanne-Joinville, J. 1957. Etudes de droit musulman malékite: les présomptions. *Revue algérienne, tunisienne et marocaine de législation et de jurisprudence*, **73**, **4**, 99–113

Lea, Henry Charles. 1974. *The Duel and the Oath*. Philadelphia: University of Pennsylvania Press [originally published 1866]

Lempert, Richard O. and Stephen A. Saltzburg. 1977. *A Modern Approach to Evidence*. St. Paul: West Publishing Co.

Levi, Edward. 1948. *An Introduction to Legal Reasoning*. Chicago: University of Chicago Press

Liebesny, Herbert J. 1975. *The Law of the Near and Middle East: Readings, Cases, and Materials*. Albany: State University of New York Press

Linant de Bellefonds, Yvon. 1965. *Traité de droit musulman comparée, Tome I: Théorie générale de l'acte juridique*. Paris: Mouton

Llewellyn, Karl. 1962. *Jurisprudence: Realism in Theory and Practice*. Chicago: University of Chicago Press

Llewellyn, Karl N. and E. Adamson Hoebel. 1941. *The Cheyenne Way*. Norman: University of Oklahoma Press

Macneil, Ian. 1985. Relational Contract: What we Do and Do Not Know. *Wisconsin Law Review*, 1985, **3**, 483–525

Mahmood, Tahir. 1972. *Family Law Reform in the Muslim World*. Bombay: N. M. Tripathi Pvt. Ltd

Makdisi, George. 1981. *The Rise of Colleges: Institutions of Learning in Islam and the West*. Edinburgh: Edinburgh University Press

Makdisi, John. 1985a. An Objective Approach to contractual Mistake in Islamic Law. *Boston University International Law Journal*, **3**, 325–44

1985b. Legal Logic and Equity in Islamic Law. *American Journal of Comparative Law*, **33**, **1**, 63–92

Malik, Imam. 1982. *Al-Muwatta*. Norwich: Diwan Press

Malinowski, Bronislaw. 1960. *A Scientific Theory of Culture and Other Essays*. Oxford: Oxford University Press

Marcy, G. 1935. Le Serment en droit coutumier berbère du Maroc central. *Renseignements Coloniaux*, 65–70

Massignon, Louis. 1952. Le Temps dans la pensée islamique. *Eranos-Jahrbuch 1951*, **20**, 141–48

Mayer, Ann E. (ed.). 1985. *Property, Social Structure and Law in the Modern Middle East*. Albany: State University of New York Press

Merryman, John Henry. 1969. *The Civil Law Tradition*. Stanford: Stanford University Press

Messick, Brinkley. 1988. Literacy and the Law: Documents and Document Specialists in Yemen. In Daisy Hilse Dwyer (ed.), *Law and Islam in the Middle East*. South Hadley, Massachusetts: Bergen and Garvey

1983. Legal Documents and the Concept of 'Restricted Literacy'. *International Journal of the Sociology of Language*, **4**, 41–52

1983b. Prosecution in Yemen: The Introduction of the Niyaba. *International Journal of Middle East Studies*, **15**, 507–18

1986. The Mufti, the Text and the World: Legal Interpretation in Yemen. *Man* (New Series), **21**, **1**, 102–19

Meyer, Leonard B. 1967. *Music, the Arts, and Ideas*. Chicago: The University of Chicago Press

Miller, Arthur Selwyn. 1984. *A "Capacity for Outrage": The Judicial Odyssey of J. Skelly Wright*. Westport, Connecticut: Greenwood Press

Milliot, Louis. 1918. *Démembrements du Habous*. Paris: Editions Leroux

1920. *Recueil de jurisprudence chérifienne, tomes I and II*. Paris: Editions Leroux

1924. *Recueil de jurisprudence chérifienne, tome III*. Paris: Editions Leroux

1953. *Introduction à l'étude du droit musulman*. Paris: Recueil Sirey

Milliot, Louis and J. Lapanne-Joinville (eds.), 1952. *Recueil de jurisprudence chérifienne*, tome IV. Paris: Librairie Recueil Sirey

Ministry of Interior, Kingdom of Saudi Arabia. 1980. *The Effect of Islamic Legislation on Crime Prevention in Saudi Arabia*. Rome: United Nations Social Defence Research Institute

Mohsen, Safia K. 1984. Islam: The Legal Dimension. In Don Peretz, Richard U. Moench, and Safia K. Mohsen, *Islam: Legacy of the Past, Challenge of the Future*. North River Press. Pp. 99–134

Moore, Sally Falk. 1978. *Law as Process: An Anthropological Approach*. London: Routledge and Kegan Paul

Morand, Marcel. 1931. *Etudes de droit musulman et de droit coutumier berbère*. Alger: Jules Carbonel

Ohio Supreme Court. 1877. *Clinton v. State*, Ohio State Reports 33:33

Pacha, A. Ibrahim. 1944. *De la responsabilité pénale en droit islamique d'après la doctrine hanafite*. Paris: T.E.P.A.C.

Percy, Walker. 1976. *The Message in the Bottle*. New York: Farrar, Strauss, and Giroux

Rabinow, Paul. 1975. *Symbolic Domination: Cultural Form and Historical Change in Morocco*. Chicago: University of Chicago Press

1977. *Reflections on Fieldwork in Morocco*. Berkeley: University of California Press

Rahman, Fazlur. 1965. *Islamic Methodology in History*. Karachi: Central Institute of Islamic Research

1968. The Status of the Individual in Islam. In Charles A. Moore (ed.), *The Status of the Individual in East and West*. Honolulu: University of Hawaii Press. Pp. 217–25

Resek, Carl. 1960. *Lewis Henry Morgan: American Scholar*. Chicago: University of Chicago Press

Rheinstein, Max. 1967. *Max Weber on Law in Economy and Society*. New York: Simon and Schuster

Rosen, Lawrence. 1968. A Moroccan Jewish Community during the Middle East Crisis. *American Scholar*, **37**, 435–51

1980–1981. Equity and Discretion in a Modern Islamic Legal System. *Law and Society Review*, **15**, **2**, 217–45

1984. *Bargaining for Reality: The Construction of Social Relations in a Muslim Community*. Chicago: University of Chicago Press

1985. Intentionality and the Concept of the Person. In J. Roland Pennock and John W. Chapman (eds.), *Criminal Justice*, NOMOS XXVII. New York: New York University Press. Pp. 52–77

1988. Islamic "Case Law" and the Logic of Consequence. In Jane Collier and June Starr (eds.), *History and Power in the Study of Law*. Ithaca: Cornell University Press

1989. Responsibility and Compensatory Justice in Arab Culture and Law. In Ben Lee and Greg Urban (eds.), *Semiotics, Self, and Society*. Berlin: Mouton

Rosenthal, Franz. 1964. Gifts and Bribes: The Muslim View. *Proceedings of the American Philosophical Society*, **108**, **2**, 135–44

Royaume du Maroc, Ministère de la Justice. 1968. *Recueil des arrêts de la Cour suprême, Chambre civile 1957–1962*. Rabat: Editions La Porte

Russell, Alexander D. and Abdullah Al-Maʿmun Suhrawardy. 1906. *First Steps in Muslim Jurisprudence*. London: Luzac

Ruthven, Malise. 1984. *Islam in the World*. London: Penguin

Ruxton, F. H. 1916. *Maliki Law*. London: Luzac
Saleh, Nabil A. 1986. *Unlawful Gain and Legitimate Profit in Islam*. Cambridge: Cambridge University Press
Sceles-Millie, J. and B. Khelifa. 1966. *Les Quatrains de Medjdoub le Sarcastique: Poète maghrébine du XVIe siècle*. Paris: G.-P. Maisonneuve at Larose
Schacht, Joseph. 1950. *Origins of Muhammadan Jurisprudence*. Oxford: Oxford University Press
    1964. *An Introduction to Islamic Law*. Oxford: Clarendon Press
    1974. Islamic Religious Law. In Joseph Schacht and C. E. Bosworth (eds.), *The Legacy of Islam*, 2nd edition. Oxford: Clarendon Press. Pp. 396–97
Scham, Alan. 1970. *Lyautey in Morocco: Protectorate Administration, 1912–1925*. Berkeley: University of California Press
Schlegel, Stuart A. 1970. *Tiruray Justice*. Berkeley: University of California Press
Schneider, David. 1980. *American Kinship: A Cultural Account*, 2nd edition. Chicago: University of Chicago Press
Shack, William A. 1979. Collective Oath: Compurgation in Anglo-Saxon England and African States. *Archives européennes de sociologie*, **20**, 1–18
Shapiro, Martin. 1981. *Courts: A Comparative and Political Analysis*. Chicago: University of Chicago Press
Smith, Wilfred Cantwell. 1965. The Concept of Shariᶜa among some Mutakallimun. In George Makdisi (ed.), *Arabic and Islamic Studies in Honor of H. A. R. Gibb*. Leiden: E. J. Brill. Pp. 581–602
Souag, Moha. 1976. La Justice et l'Injustice. *Lamalif*, no. 83 (October), 41
Starr, June. 1978. *Dispute and Settlement in Rural Turkey*. Leiden: E. J. Brill
Steiner, Joseph M. 1976. Judicial Discretion and the Concept of Law. *Cambridge Law Journal*, **35**, 1, 135–57
Steingass, F. (trans.). 1898. *The Assemblies of Al Hariri*, vol. II. London: Royal Asiatic Society
Toledano, Henry. 1981. *Judicial Practice and Family Law in Morocco*. Boulder and New York: Social Science Monographs and Columbia University Press
Turner, Bryan S. 1974. *Weber and Islam: A Critical Study*. London: Routledge and Kegan Paul
Turner, Victor. 1969. *The Ritual Process*. London: Routledge and Kegan Paul
    1982. *From Ritual to Theatre*. New York: Performing Arts Journal Publications
Tyan, Emile. 1926. *Le Système de responsabilité délictuelle en droit musulman*. Beirut: Imprimerie Catholique.
    1945. *Le Notariat et le régime de la preuve par écrit dans la pratique du droit musulman*. Beirut: Université de Lyon, Annales de l'Ecole Française de Droit de Beyrouth
    1960. *Histoire de l'organisation judiciaire en pays d'Islam*. Leiden: E. J. Brill
Tylor, Edward B. 1871. *Primitive Culture*. London: John Murray
Udovitch, A. 1985. Islamic Law and the Social Context of Exchange in the Medieval Middle East. *History and Anthropology*, **1**, 445–65
Ungar, Roberto. 1986. *The Critical Legal Studies Movement*. Cambridge, Massachusetts: Harvard University Press
United States Supreme Court. 1949. *Terminiello v. Chicago*, United States Reports 337: 11
Université de Rabat, Faculté des Sciences Juridiques Economiques et Sociales. 1961. *Recueil des arrêts de la Cour suprême, Chambre criminelle 1957–60*. Rabat: Editions La Porte

Wakin, Jeanette A. 1972. *The Function of Documents in Islamic Law*. Albany: State University of New York Press
Wehr, Hans. 1976. *A Dictionary of Modern Written Arabic*. Edited by J. Milton Cowan. Ithaca: Cornell University Press
Weissbourd, Bernard and Elizabeth Mertz. 1985. Rule-Centrism versus Legal Creativity: The Skewing of Legal Ideology through Language. *Law and Society Review*, **19**, **4**, 623–60
Westermarck, Edward. 1947. Customs Connected with Homicide in Morocco. *Transactions of the Westermarck Society*, **1**, 7–38
White, James Boyd. 1973. *The Legal Imagination*. Boston: Little, Brown; abridged edition, University of Chicago Press, 1985
Wigmore, John Henry. 1936. *A Panorama of the World's Legal Systems*. Washington, DC: Washington Law Book Co.
    1941. *A Kaleidoscope of Justice*. Washington, DC: Washington Law Book Co.
Yamani, Ahmad Zaki. 1968. *Islamic Law and Contemporary Issues*. Jidda: The Saudi Publishing House
Zeys, E. and Mohammed Ould Sidi Said. 1946. *Recueil d'actes et de judgements arabes*. Alger: Editions Jules Carbonel
Ziadeh, Farhat J. 1960. 'Urf and Law in Islam. In James Kritzeck and R. Bayley Winder (eds.), *The World of Islam*. London: Macmillan. Pp. 60–67
Zirari-Devif, Michèle. 1979. La Fonction pénale du juge communal. *Revue juridique, politique et economique du Maroc*, **5**, 79–93

Index

of taking, 33–35; in western law, 32, 33

ordeals, 35

party wall case, 29–30
paternity, 45
physiognomy: science of, 24, 45, 78
plaintiff and defendant, *see* oaths: order of taking
polygamy, 63
population: Muslims in world, xv
presumptions, 28–31, 34, 43–44, 48–49; *see also* legal reasoning
probability, 77
procedure, 7–10
property disputes, 8, 48–49
Prophet Muhammad, 23, 25, 41, 42

qadi (Islamic judge), 3; bias of, 10; goal of, 17–18, 41, 43, 55–56, 61; as religious official, 9, 10, 65; social background of, 65; western images of, 18–19, 58–59
qadi's court: description of, 6–11
qiyas (analogic reasoning), 42
Quran, 10, 27, 41–42, 43, 48, 54, 60; literacy and, 41

rajih (preferred opinion), 47
Reisman, David, 2
responsibility, 54, 78
ritual, 16, 36

sacrifice, 16
sales, 43
Saudi Arabia, 52, 68
Sefrou, 6, 62, 64, 65

Seldon, John, 68
shari'a (Islamic law), *see* Islamic law
sin, 51
social identity, 7–10, 12–13, 25, 44–45, 52–55, 60
social relations: negotiation of, 11–14, 15, 16–18, 22, 37, 43, 50, 54, 56–57, 60, 66; quest for information about, 13, 14
social utility, 47–49
Stein, Gertrude, 51

Tamm, Judge Edward, 69
time: concept of, 14–15, 54
Traditions of the Prophet, 23, 41–42, 51, 60
tribe, 11, 15
truth, 13, 22, 24–25, 35, 50
Tunisia, 63
Tylor, E. B., 35

United States Supreme Court, 58
unjust enrichment, 60, 61, 66, 67, 76
usury, *see* unjust enrichment

Weber, Max, 35, 59–60, 65
Williams, Edward Bennett, 69–70
witnesses, 7–10, 17, 21–23, 42; assessment in court of, 25; certification of, 24; neighbors as, 25, 28–30; notaries' interrogation of, 9, 11; relatives as, 9, 10, 25, 28; required number of, 24–25
women: legal rights and powers of, 7–10, 26; statutory period for pregnancy of, 30
Wright, Judge J. Skelly, 69–73